# YOU® BRAND

# YOU® BRAND

## Advance your Career by Building a Personal Brand

Veronica Canning

Published in 2014 by
Chartered Accountants Ireland
Chartered Accountants House
47–49 Pearse Street
Dublin 2
www.charteredaccountants.ie

This publication is designed to provide accurate and authoritative information in regard to the subject matter covered. It is provided on the understanding that The Institute of Chartered Accountants in Ireland is not engaged in rendering professional services. The Institute of Chartered Accountants in Ireland disclaims all liability for any reliance placed on the information contained within this publication and recommends that if professional advice or other expert assistance is required, the services of a competent professional should be sought.

All persons named in this book as examples or in illustrative stories are fictitious; no real persons' names are used and any resemblance to real persons, living or dead, is entirely coincidental.

ISBN 978-1-908199-76-8

Typeset by Compuscript
Printed by Turner's Printing Company, Longford, Ireland

*To Peter, Amber and Chris*

# Contents

# Acknowledgements

I would like to thank all the people that I have worked with over the years and from whom I have learnt so much.

My family were with me at every stage of writing this book and gave me great insights along the way and on every aspect.

I would not have finished this book without the help of my friend Leanne, who helped with her incredible advice and support.

The publishing team at Chartered Accountants Ireland were marvellous, especially Lisa and Michael, whose input and editing vastly improved the clarity and style of the final book.

I had help from a range of people who read the many drafts and very generously shared their experience and insights. Specifically, I would like to thank Dermot, Genevieve, Amber, Peter, Geraldine and Leanne for their suggestions.

I would also like to thank all the staff at Monart for making the long stretches of writing so easy in their little piece of heaven in Wexford, especially their wonderful managers, Mark and Patrick.

# Personal branding and its role in your career success

*"Life isn't about finding yourself. Life is about creating yourself."*
George Bernard Shaw

® **Understand your personal brand**
® **You® personal brand model**

## What will you be famous for?

I recently gave a speech to the women of a large consultancy firm that was holding a one-day session to kick off their mentorship programme for women. They were committed to supporting more women in getting to the top of their organisation, and asked me to give a thought-provoking address to encourage the women to ask the panel of partners and senior leaders probing questions about mentoring, and what they planned for them, the firm's future leaders.

I decided to describe the scene as I, an outsider, saw it. I said that I noticed that when young people join these big organisations it is akin to the experience of joining a tribe. It looks fabulous from the outside, full of super-smart people in a dynamic and competitive environment where there is an opportunity to make a name for yourself and earn lots of money. However, once inside you realise that the tribe has clear rules and rituals and is quick to expel those who don't fit in.

> I'm reminded of the BBC TV series about meerkats called *Meerkat Manor*, filmed in South Africa. 'Flower' was the name of the female meerkat who rose to lead the 'mob' or 'clan' and her progress through all the stages is seen in the series. *Meerkat Manor* reflects brilliantly on human rituals and how you need to follow tribal rules or you are out. It belongs in the world of strange tales where the world of nature mimics the human world, as in my experience this set-up is comparable with the corporate world.

I opened my speech by observing that, as women in this company, they were in the top 5% of Irish women: they excelled at school, excelled in college, excelled in their Master's degrees and were, in fact, the pick of the crop. They had passed the stringent recruitment process in a buyer's market. They had got through the internal cattle market process, and now here they were, all bright and shiny, impressive and ready to climb the corporate ladder.

Alas, there were so many of them and they were all very impressive. They were at the bottom of a pyramid with a very pointy top. Only a few of them were going to make it to the top of this organisation, this 'tribe'. I asked them whether they'd thought about what was going to make them stand out from such an impressive group of peers. Asked another way: "What are you going to be famous for?" I left them in no doubt that those who figured out the answer to that question stood the greatest chance of success.

It is no different for you. "What am I going to be famous for, and how am I going to achieve it?" is the question you need to ask if you want to stand out. You will stand out through your unique personal brand.

## What is a personal brand?

Your personal brand is what others say about you. Remember one important principle: your personal brand is not what *you* say it is, it's what *others* say it is, what others say about you. My definition of a personal brand is: "What they say about you when you leave the room". You know what I mean; usually, the description is short, pointed and deadly accurate. Irish people are good with words, and there's none better when putting someone down.

Your personal brand is a definer of success in your career as it is the most visible marker of you and what you stand for and, as such, it offers you the chance to take control of what people say about you in a corporate setting. It gives you a distinct advantage in having an active input into building your career.

Listen well the next time you hear the side comments after a meeting, especially when someone has been upset. How many times have you sat in a room and heard someone being written off with one sentence, or heard someone else being damned with faint praise? Whether or not you believe you have a brand, such comments constitute it. Think of the most memorable descriptions that you have heard. Remember that a similar comment could be attached to you. Often admiration is expressed in few words, like: 'rising star', 'jet-propelled', 'one to watch', 'born gentleman', or 'straight as a die'.

## Your personal brand is either accidental or purposeful

Everyone has a personal brand; it's not something you can opt out of. It is inevitable, but the good news is that you can control whether yours is 'purposeful' or 'accidental'. A crucial point is that what your brand looks and feels like is up to you! I believe that when you take control of all aspects of your personal brand, you craft a purposeful one that is authentic and is an integral part of your career plan. In addition, a purposeful brand is considerably more likely to be a *positive* one, as you will see as you read on.

I often say this to audiences when speaking at conferences, and I see the odd sceptical face, but when I ask them if their personal brand is accidental or purposeful, the scepticism disappears. They move to questioning which kind of personal brand they have. It is an enlightening moment when you realise that every day people are interacting with you and judging you by your appearance, accent, behaviours, moods and by your impact on them. If you are unaware of this and just do and say what you want, as you want, without reference to those around you, you definitely do not have a purposeful personal brand.

## Four core truths about your personal brand

Exploring your personal brand begins with these four hard-core truths:

### 1. You are at the centre of your personal brand

The number one truth is that *you* are at the centre of your personal brand. It is built on you and your values, it emanates from you, it is played out by your behaviours. For it to succeed and contribute to your development it must be authentic. You may think you can fake it; like the person who asks everyone how they are and wants to look like they care, but then rosters them on long hours, or ignores requests to take leave for important occasions like weddings and funerals. They fake that they are good people managers and care about their staff, but their deeds show that all they care about is results. You may be good at faking it, but believe me, others will eventually see the real you. The inconsistency between the two is surprisingly visible to observers. It is often given away in subliminal ways and expressed as a feeling or intuition. There is a dissonance, and observers catch it. Someone will express a fear that the person "is not all they seem to be", or "there is something off about that person" and the result is an *accidental* brand, not a purposeful one.

## 2. You are in charge of your current and future personal brand

You create your brand daily, and you are responsible for it. Every action you take further defines it. It is vital that you realise that it is not an optional extra that you may get to later, when you are happy, wealthy and wise. It is a big part of you now, at this moment. There is no point blaming your colleagues or your boss if you are in difficulty at work; you are a key player in your own drama. Often, when I work with people who hate their job and everyone they work with, they see the answer as leaving so they can start afresh in a new place. I always remind them that the unfortunate reality is that they take themselves with them to the new job. It's far too easy to blame everyone else when you are the problem.

## 3. It is your single biggest transportable asset

As people move away from having a job for life, or being a 'lifer' in one company, and move to having a career made up of different parts – jobs, periods of transition, breaks for education or child care and, increasingly, periods of unemployment – your brand becomes your most valuable transportable asset. In an increasingly fluid workplace, you have to move to a 'portfolio' approach to your career. You are the only constant as you move through a career spanning decades. You therefore need to concentrate on imagining yourself as a little enterprise, 'You Incorporated', with unique skills, competencies and a personal brand.

## 4. It is a vibrant, evolving part of you

The core 'you' remains more or less the same, but your confidence, experience, self-knowledge, projection and the extent of your *fame* changes. You will not have the same personal brand as a mid-level executive as, later, a successful senior executive – at least I hope you won't.

The key message is that you have a brand at every stage, and as you learn from your mistakes you will continuously adjust it. The great thing about getting older is that although you keep making mistakes, they are different ones, and you avoid repeating the disasters of the earlier part of your career.

## Brands are emotional

I notice that when my friends talk about brands, they do so with emotion: "I love my Audi"; "I only wear Jo Malone perfume"; "Guinness is the only beer worth drinking"; "I love the prices in Penneys". Brands depend on and exploit your emotional engagement with the very idea of them. When pressed to explain this emotional attachment, you find yourself starting off rationally and then you reach down to the emotion. You start saying things like "I love it", "I enjoy it", I like being seen in it", or "I always buy it because I trust it".

Now, take a step back from your favourite brands and stay in that mindset as you begin to look at your personal brand. You also have this emotional effect on others! Your personal brand engages with those around you on an emotional level and can have a positive or a negative effect on people. You've heard of the "Marmite effect", when a brand provokes a strong reaction, good or bad. I hear about it every day. As we become more stressed in our daily lives, moderate views are replaced and we are more vocal about the brands we love or hate. This book will help you discover your personal brand and take firm control of it.

## How to build your brand: the eight steps

It's easy to think that working hard will get you noticed and promoted. If only it were that easy. I know for certain that it won't. If you adopt the strategy of putting the head down, working like crazy and hoping the boss will notice and reward, you are likely suffering from 'Good Worker Syndrome'.

You need to be crystal clear on what makes a *noticeable* personal brand before you set about building it. I believe everyone is capable of building a really purposeful, powerful personal brand and I will give you the road map and the key ingredients to do so. While success or failure will be tangible, the achievement of it will be the result of what's in your head; the key consideration for you is to develop the belief that you can do it!

I want to give you the biggest challenge ever. Why be good when you could be outstanding? I want to challenge you to transform your personal brand, to elevate it, to aim for true impact.

As illustrated in the figure below, I have developed a 'Personal Brand Model' that follows the **Eight Steps** outlined in this book. Below is an overview before you begin working through each of them.

**YOU® PERSONAL BRAND MODEL:**
**EIGHT STEPS TO BUILDING YOUR PERSONAL BRAND**

### Step 1: Build self-knowledge: look inside

The starting point in developing your personal brand is how well you know yourself. How accurate is your self-reflective lens?

As your personal brand comes from within, your authentic self always shows through. I start every personal brand development programme with the person working to discover insights into their personality. This is the starting point to building an authentic personal brand. You cannot shape someone into something they are not. You just need to think of some recent examples of meltdowns of celebrities when a carefully crafted personal brand imploded because it was not authentic.

The key is to find out the driving force underpinning your personality, as it shapes your view of the world. Examples of *driving forces* are the need to always be helpful, the need to be right, the need for perfection. (Drivers are discussed in more detail in Step 5.) You behave in reaction to your perception. It can be a surprise to discover that your understanding of a situation is unique and not shared by anyone else.

Constant self-evaluation is needed as you change jobs, roles, companies, teams, because, as your role changes and the people around you change, you need to adapt. Some people are intransigent and insist that "what you see is what you get". They stubbornly stay the same. My question for them is always: "How is that working for you, then?" Embracing the uncomfortable reality that you may need to change is an important part of the self-discovery process.

In Step 1 you will be shown how to work through the levels of the self-discovery process and, at the end, pull together all the insights to get a clear self-view.

## Step 2: Build self-knowledge: look around you

In Step 2 you look outside of yourself and understand others' perception of you. This deepens your self-knowledge and can be a transforming exercise. Based on all your insights you are then able to see clearly your personal strengths and successes. At the end of these two steps you can develop your personal brand statement.

## Step 3: Build your future career

In taking this third step, the question you need to ask yourself is: do you have a clear idea of your career plan? It is not possible to build a personal brand in isolation from your work life and your career plans. I have read books that give advice and techniques to build personal brand, but in isolation from any investigation of your actual work life. I believe that techniques and approaches to improve your personal brand work considerably better if used in real time and with your real career.

Before we go into all the aspects of planning your career, I would like you to start the process by asking yourself some basic questions:
- Do you think you have a job or do you see yourself as having a career?
- Do you have a career plan?
- Do you have milestones in your career plan?
- Do you know which milestone you are at in your career?
- Are you drifting along, just reacting to events in work without any real plan?
- Are you actually where you want to be and doing what you want to do?

In Step 3 you move on to develop an intensive insight into your career ambition and decide on your 'Big Audacious Aim' and how to align it with your personal brand.

## Step 4: Develop outstanding brand skills and behaviours

In Step 1 you looked at yourself in detail; in this step you look at something different. You look at the behaviours people see in you on a daily basis. At the root of your personal brand lies your behaviour. It is by your actions that you are known. Do you know how your everyday behaviour constantly feeds into the changing perception of you? Do you understand which of your behaviours has the potential to seriously damage your personal brand?

In this step, you examine your skills and behaviours and how they add to or detract from your personal brand every day, under the following main impression points which define and redefine your impact on others:

- good or bad first impressions;
- communication skills;
- leadership skills;
- adding value to the business.

Step 4 will give you valuable advice on how to turn these impression points to your advantage.

## Step 5: Don't let your drivers derail you

Progressing further into your behaviour, in Step 5 you decide if any of your personality drivers that have delivered success to date, have (if overused) become a weakness and begun to 'derail you'.

Each of us has a defining driving behaviour: you like to deliver results; you're a listener; you're vigilant and cautious. The key question is "Will the behaviour that got me here get me to the next level?". Step 5 will move your understanding of your behaviour to a whole new level. It will allow you to recognise any behaviour that has served you well to date, but might, if overplayed, actually *derail* your personal brand. Many people I work with who have damaged personal brands have suffered from this phenomenon of being derailed by just one out-of-control behaviour.

## Step 6: Hold your power

Finally, you'll discover in Step 6 if, despite having developed a successful personal brand, you may be 'leaking power' in certain key situations, halting your further progress. Step 6 explains the concept of leaking power and how it can damage you, and advises on how to hold your power.

Have you noticed how you can have a great personal brand and still have difficulty? It's as if you are damaging yourself by leaking your power to someone or something else. I often ask this question when I am giving talks on personal branding, as I am convinced that it is not a well-known concept. You can work very hard on your personal brand, consider it to be in great shape and then suddenly feel you have lost it. Over the years I have worked with people who change and seem to lose their zest over a short period of time. It can be because they have become trapped in a poor view of themselves, developed a victim mindset, or it can be through their own, often unconscious, behaviours.

It can happen at some transition point: a new job, a new boss or a new colleague, usually something that has forced a change in their circumstances or behaviours, or both. Sometimes your environment takes on a new dimension, becomes 'wicked', as explained in Step 6, but you are still behaving as if nothing new had happened.

When discussing Step 6 in detail I explain this concept and how to stop leaking power and become good at holding onto it. I see three main ways in which you can leak power:
• through your mindset;
• through your behaviour;
• in wicked environments.

## Step 7: Take your personal brand to work: your matrix

The crucial next stage for you is to look at where you operate your personal brand, the corporate playing field, which I call the 'matrix'. By this I mean having an excellent understanding of the hierarchy in which you work. Is it many-layered, horizontal, all in one place or scattered across the globe? Do you know who has influence over your career? Do you have a good relationship with them? More basically, do the right people know you exist and are you influencing what they think of you?

This is the point at which you bring your personal brand out to play! You are always working away on your personal brand, but at some point you have to look around you and get real about the workplace in which you find yourself. I observe people studying how to manage people in their teams, but not enough attention is paid to the art of 'managing up'. By this I mean how you build relationships with your superiors, manage their expectations of you and manage the impression you are making on them, or manage their effect on your career. How good are you at that? It could be the most important part of succeeding in your career. Step 7 is about how to understand the matrix and what you need to do to be astute in your navigation of the corporate world.

## Step 8: Position your brand for the future

Finally, there is the realisation that you need to get out there and make yourself known. Are you working away in your silo and getting the job done with a shorter-term job view, or are you looking around you and taking a long-term career view? Do you network both in and out of the company? Do you have connections with powerful people who will advise you? The workplace is too harsh a place today and too competitive to leave your career to chance; you need to proactively position yourself where the right people will see you shine. Step 8 will tell you all about this and tempt you to engage in advanced positioning strategies.

Before we begin working through the eight steps of the model, I want to first tell you a story about someone and how he discovered, almost too late, what was shaping his personal brand. (I have not used real names, and the details of situations and circumstances described in similar stories in this book have been altered.)

### ADAM: A REAL PERSONAL BRAND STORY

I once worked with a young man called Adam, who was referred to me by his boss, Michael. They worked in the local office of a global company.

Adam was described as "wilful, opinionated and not willing to take advice". His boss said that Adam had "gone off the rails" and he was not sure he could even begin to rescue his career.

It transpired that he had recently been asked to lead a major outsourcing project in an emerging region for the company and was seconded for six months to deliver the result needed. One of the corporate vice presidents was Michael's corporate sponsor (who had sponsored this project). So this assignment was a visible indicator of how well Michael's team could deliver.

Adam was to kick ass and get results. He was pre-programmed with a lot of macho management instructions, like: "we focus on results"; "make these people respect you"; "the only way is to lead from the top". He believed what he was told, and he went out to fight like a gladiator entering the arena.

To fully understand this story you need to know about Adam. He is a results-orientated person, so much so that his sense of self-worth is entwined with being seen to deliver expected outcomes success-fully. To date he has delivered, but in the company's home market and under close observation and supervision. This delivery contri-buted to the decision to send him on this 'stretch' assignment.

Adam seeks and gets affirmation through producing the best work. He sees praise for his achievements as personal praise. He has a vested interest in succeeding in work. He does not do failure; it's too harmful to his sense of self-worth.

So Adam went and worked flat-out for six months, immersing him-self in the detail and totally focusing on the instruction to deliver the project on time and on budget. He had been told it was his big chance to prove himself and to impress head office.

While he was there, he combined his results-driven approach with the boss's instruction to deliver a flawless project. He took to heart the concept that he was proving himself, and that he needed to impress. He was like an astronaut gone off into space, with all the resources he needed in his Apollo rocket. He believed that he was self-sufficient and could deliver without any supervision.

Adam focused on the end result, and his behaviour was orientated to deliver at whatever cost. He drove the team relentlessly, laid down the law and brooked no disagreement. When more expe-rienced voices cautioned him, he ignored them as he understood that he was proving himself, not looking for advice.

He concentrated on his performance, the impression he needed to make, and when something outside his experience came up he felt that he could not ask for advice, so he guessed what to do. He felt that he couldn't check back with base. After all, he couldn't show his inexperience or lack of skills. He is not naturally arrogant, but his insecurity bred arrogance.

The impact of his behaviour took a while to show up at Michael's desk. Slowly, he began to hear grumbling, then the emails of complaint started to flow in, slowly at first but then a flood of them. The team all complained about Adam and how he was behaving. Finally, people even began to refuse to work with him!

He had left with the personal brand of an "up-and-coming go-getter" and came home with the personal brand of "wilful, opinionated and not willing to take advice".

## What went wrong with Adam?

Adam crashed and burned. He had listened to what was asked of him, internalised it, but the problem arose when he aligned his boss's aims with his internal drive to deliver results and succeed at any cost.

Adam explained his side of the story to me. He understood that he was the one responsible for the outcomes. He felt that he had been dispatched and told to take charge. He drove the team as instructed, took decisions as instructed, delivered on time as instructed, stayed in budget as instructed. He could not see the problem. Yet he knew he was in deep trouble.

He failed to see that the way you behave is as important as the results you achieve.

His boss, Michael, explained that Adam went off on a tangent, listened to no one, was too 'bolshie' to ask for guidance, hid things, alienated the local team, and generally let him down. Michael had no realisation of the pressure he had put Adam under and no understanding that he had failed to correctly orientate him or support him in a consistent way. Both men felt let down by the other. It was personal on both sides and trust and respect were obliterated.

When I met Adam he was tearful and very chastened by the whole, terrible experience. He had lost all confidence in his own ability.

On his return he was demoted a grade and sent to the back wall of the large open-plan office; the equivalent of the loo paper section of the government stationery office. My first job was in the Department of Finance and the threat of being sent to "The Stationery Office" has stuck in my brain. That threat was often spoken of as a caution to young wilful graduates like me, who entered the traditional, slow-moving civil service of the time. If you did not learn the rules of the tribe and how to compromise, you would be counting loo rolls.

## Let's examine Adam's personal brand

Now look at these questions and consider how different Adam's experience might have been if he had asked them:

- What was really expected of me? Did I really understand the whole situation?
- Did I ask enough questions before I left?
- Did I reflect on what was really going on?
- Did I realise how much my boss's personal brand was invested in the success of this?
- Why did I forget office politics?
- What were the hidden agendas?
- Why did I take such a narrow view?
- Why was I blind to other people's input?
- How much did my pride drive me?
- Was I afraid of being discovered as being out of my depth and why did I not ask for help?
- Why did my courage fail me, and why did I not ask Michael for help before I got into difficulty?
- Did I stop and think of the effect of my behaviours?
- Did I realise that my personal brand was on show and under close scrutiny?

The main insight this story offers is that Adam had no idea he had a personal brand, or that it was under close scrutiny by senior people while he was away on assignment. He realised when we had worked together what his missteps had been, and he was able to rebuild his personal brand.

## And Adam now?

You will be delighted to know that Adam is back from the wall. We worked for eight months on repairing his personal brand; we did a thorough examination of his personal brand and crafted a new one. He is now once again spoken of as "one to watch", and this time he really is.

The process that I took Adam and many others through is outlined in this book to give you insight into how you can begin to build a purposeful personal brand that will ensure your success.

# Step 1

## Build self-knowledge: look inside

*"Be yourself, everyone else is already taken."*

Oscar Wilde

® **Self-knowledge is fundamental**
® **The self-discovery process**
® **How to pull all the insights together**

## Self-knowledge is fundamental

To build a personal brand you *must* start with self-knowledge, which is why I have devoted a whole step for introducing you to it and equipping you to develop it. People starting this process often want to rush into the fun work associated with building an excellent personal brand, but I restrain them until they have first done the hard work of understanding themselves.

I want you to do the same. Pause and have a good look at yourself using all the resources of this step. Why? Well, you are the basis on which we will build your personal brand. You can't build a personal brand in isolation from your personality, inner drives, strengths and foibles. I see people trying to develop one without self-knowledge and I watch how the cracks instantly appear because the average person has an uncanny knack for detecting lack of authenticity.

## It's not what you *think* about yourself that matters ...

It is not about what you *think* of yourself, it's about what you *know* about yourself. You are the only one inside your skin and yet you can have the most difficulty in understanding yourself. Others can see you in a more detached way because of their objective viewpoint; they see your personality in every interaction with you. You may be unaware of it, but they are forming opinions of you all the time and can describe you accurately in a few devastating words. You need to become a detached and informed observer of yourself.

In the international bestseller, *Thinking Fast and Slow* (Penguin, 2011), Nobel Prize-winner Daniel Kahneman says:

> "The notion that we have limited access to the workings of our minds is difficult to accept because, naturally, it is alien to our experience, but it is true: you know far less about yourself than you feel you do."

### Famous last words: "I am who I am"

I am amazed at the number of people I meet who utter the immortal phrase, "I am who I am, I expect people to take me as they find me". To me this statement is a hallmark of a lack of self-exploration and self-awareness, so I always question it, which takes such people aback, as they don't actually realise that this stance might be a lost opportunity.

### I can be who you want me to be: who do you want today?

Some of us have a tendency to adapt ourselves to the person we are with, and because of these interactions we have different personalities in different circumstances, but that can be quite superficial as the real personality is hidden underneath.

What you project to others is a key element of your personal brand. People with little self-knowledge are usually the owners of *accidental* brands; they have no idea of who they are or what they are projecting.

### Beware the 'negativity warp' effect

Being surrounded by a negative atmosphere and negative people will adversely affect you. So be careful about the amount of time you spend with very negative people as they can warp your outlook. I call people who are constantly negative and destructive in their outlook 'psychic vampires'; you know them by their determination to see the worst in everything and by their need to put people down at every chance. The best strategy to lessen their effect is to remove yourself; I recommend you run, if you can.

### I already know myself

You need to know the most potent influencers of your behaviour, your hot spots, and your vulnerabilities. They are the hidden influencers of your personal brand.

Although this may seem an obvious step, in my experience a lot of people find it very difficult. They consider themselves too busy or too important to stop and think. With each day that I observe more and more executives in action, I realise that self-deception is common and drives a lot of bad workplace behaviours.

Self-exploration can be challenging for successful people who have never had to engage in this kind of thinking before. Stick with it and be honest with yourself; if you really don't know where to start, ask a trusted advisor outside the organisation for some guidance to get you started. Learning about yourself is a hard task; it requires introspection, inquiry and some honesty. I have observed an inverse ratio in operation on this issue: the people with the least knowledge of themselves are often the most resistant to any discovery process. I have seen grown men throw tantrums when presented with the need to understand themselves.

## Know what people are saying about you

Let's start at the obvious places to look for what people are saying about you:
- Annual appraisals
- Feedback sessions
- 360-degree evaluation
- Staff turnover, absenteeism.

I am surprised by how people fail to notice the clear messages about their personal brands in these routine interactions. Don't automatically blame those around you. Look at yourself first.

As many of the above take place in a formal setting, it can be useful to ask questions about your performance in informal relaxed settings, as people are more inclined to be honest then. You can find out a lot in chats with the boss when she gives you hints, you just need to be alert to them.

### Look at the behaviour of people around you for clues

Your personal brand is very obvious to those close to you. They see you all day, every day, and so see all your moods, not just you on your best behaviour. Observe them with these questions in mind:
- Do they feel free to ask me questions?
- Do they share the real situation with me or do they only give me good news?
- Do they feel sure enough of me to challenge my opinions?
- Do I check their body language? How much eye contact do they make with me?
- Do they seem happy to see me approach them?
- Do they genuinely respect me as a person or do they respect my authority because of my position?
- Do they exclude me? Go around me, undermine me?

## The self-discovery process

To arrive at a place where you have good self-knowledge you have to go through a questioning process, which I call 'the self-discovery process'.

Let's start your self-discovery process with the most obvious and easiest questions you can ask yourself. As you read through these questions and the explanations, it might help you to mark the situation that best describes you. This will help when we come back to pull together all your conclusions about yourself.

### Self-discovery: level 1 – outlook

#### Are you a negative or a positive person?

I think there is a spectrum, with 'Pollyannas' on one end and highly negative people, 'negatroids', on the other. Where are you most of the time? As you go about your work every day, are you viewing what happens to you in a positive or a negative way? Do you always look for the positives in a situation, encouraging your team with the positive outcome, even when they are in the middle of a difficult situation?

Or do you moan and bring everyone's mood down? Like when the team discovers there is a problem and everyone has to stay in all night to get it sorted, do you point out that they are missing the best party of the year? Are you always pointing out the problems? Was the phrase "glass half empty" invented for you? Has anyone told you that that is your view of the world? Think carefully because you can be certain people are aware if you are living on one end of this particular spectrum. Note for yourself where you think you mostly reside on the spectrum.

| Negative | Balanced | Positive |
|---|---|---|

A 'balanced' person can also be called an "optimistic realist", which connects us to the next question.

### Are you an optimist or a pessimist?

You may not realise it, but we all tend to default into one or other category. The answer is obvious when you ask yourself how you receive and process good and bad news. When you get bad news, do you think this is just more of the same bad news that life dishes out to you, or that this is a random event? When you get good news do you think that is the norm for you or just a random event?

If you are an optimist then you have a core belief that good things happen most of the time and you see that as 'normal'. You believe that bad things happen only now and again and that bad things are not the norm for you. A pessimist has the opposite view, believing that bad things happen to them all the time, are their fate, and that good things are random and unexpected.

Where do you fall? Don't automatically say you are in the middle, think hard about it. I have discovered in workshops that participants will often duck this exercise and instantly say they're in the middle, even though I know from listening to their previous contributions that they are very negative people. So really think about this and be honest. This viewpoint has an effect on your outlook and how you behave in your career. If you believe that bad things are always going to be there to damage your career, you will give up more easily. People who do not succumb to helplessness are buoyed up because they believe bad things are only temporary.

Listen to people around you as they discuss the company's outlook, job prospects or possibilities of career progression, and spot the pessimists. Note their vocabulary, their stories, quite a lot of them are like

Chicken Little, the infamous chicken hero of the folktale who goes around telling everyone the sky is falling down, just because he was hit on the head by an acorn. Ask yourself: just how much of a Chicken Little are you? If you establish that you're a pessimist, it's important to try to work around your tendencies toward catastrophic thinking and to strive to become an optimist.

The more you tell yourself that bad things are the norm, the more you veer towards helplessness; the more you take the view that bad things are temporary and will pass, the more you access *resilience.*

### How much do you let bad news affect all aspects of your life?

Do you take each setback so hard that you allow it to affect every single aspect of you? Do you contain it in the part of your life where it arises, or do you let it seep into all aspects of your life? If you get a negative end-of-year assessment in work do you see it as an aspect of your work life, or do you let it affect your whole life, including relationships with family and friends?

I see people who 'awfulise' (or 'catastrophise') the situation. They cannot put a piece of bad news aside and continue to be positive in other parts of their life; they let it affect their mood, outlook on life, sometimes even their whole future. They allow having a bad time in work ruin their home life and put them into a black hole. To avoid this, try this approach: when something bad happens, aim to see it as a stand-alone occurrence that you can compartmentalise, and meanwhile continue to see the many other parts of your life as unaffected by it, and be happy. If you see the negative event in a general and pervasive way, it can permeate and affect all aspects of your life. Note for yourself where you think you mostly reside on this compartmentalise/catastrophise spectrum.

| Pessimist | Balanced | Optimist |
| --- | --- | --- |

I have been very influenced by Martin Seligman, and his work on positive psychology. If you read any of his works you can learn about optimism and pessimism in greater detail. I really like his book *Flourish: A Visionary New Understanding of Happiness and Well-being* (Free Press, 2011).

### Self-discovery: level 2 – find your prime motivator

Now that you have some sight of your level of basic positivity and optimism, let's have a look at what might be motivating you. As you read this section, circle the scenarios that most resonate with you. See which of these motivations drives your behaviour:

- Looking for approval
- Fear
- Having lots of options
- Expressing strong feelings
- Preferring to see others' points of view.

### Are you looking for approval?

Most of us like to be told we are wonderful or at least doing a great job. But for some people, seeking and gaining approval is hard-wired into their psyche.

Have a look at these three questions and see if they resonate with you.

1. How much do you seek the approval of people around you? When you are supervising people, do you find it difficult to clearly spell out what you require of them? Are you coaxing and nudging them to do your bidding? Do you complain about their performance behind their back, but then don't have the courage to really make your demands clear, even though you are their boss? Are you the agreeable, helpful boss? Do people describe you as nice? Is it possible that you are a pushover? Do you always look to connect with people and make yourself indispensable to them? How much do you factor ways to please the boss into your planning for meetings? How much do you let your need to be agreeable run your management behaviours?

   If you find yourself putting others' preferences first and not ever getting what you need done, you may be prioritising their approval before all else.

   | No, this is not me | Yes, this is me |
   | --- | --- |

2. How much does approval for your work and your results matter to you? Are you constantly conscious of how you appear to others, especially those you need to impress? If you do, you probably always finish your projects so as to appear to be in control. You have little tolerance of others making you look bad; you get angry if the poor work of others lets the team down, and you take other people's lack of attention to detail personally. If you like to get approval for your stellar work, you focus on getting things done on time and to the highest standards. However, you worry less about *how* you get things done, or how hard you work and the pressure you put people under, than you do about the need to produce the results.

If you recognise this, you may be a top performer when results matter above all else, but you could be running into difficulty in keeping people working for you. You simply wear them out. You probably also wear yourself out but are happy the work is done. Work/life balance may also be an issue.

| No, this is not me | Yes, this is me |
|---|---|

3. When you meet someone or enter a new situation, do you immediately compare yourself to the others to see if you are good enough? Some people have a constant tendency to feel uneasy about how they are measuring up. They approach new situations with mental balancing scales. They are on edge, judging, balancing themselves against the people they meet. An internal dialogue takes place asking some version of the following questions: Am I as intelligent? Am I as well-dressed? Am I as good? Am I as experienced as this person? The underlying thrust of these questions is a fear that you are not good enough.

If you recognise this, then this may be a real constraint on your ability to flourish, principally because you may try to compensate for feeling unequal with some form of a put-down to equal the odds. If you do this, you will be known for it, and your feeling of inadequacy may be misinterpreted as you being unpleasant.

It's perfectly alright to measure yourself against others, but the question for you here is how often you do this. If this is a constant, then you need to note it and try to counteract it. Lack of confidence may be an issue for you.

| No, this is not me | Yes, this is me |
|---|---|

## Is fear ruling your life?

Fear plays a part in all of our lives, but some people are able to overcome it or ignore it, and it does not become a driving force. For others it plays a big part, a definer of behaviour in some instances.

Have a look at the following questions and see what part, if any, fear plays in your life.

1. Are you trying too hard and chasing perfection so as not to fail? Are you someone who likes to have every little last detail right? Do you see 99% of a project completed and hold everything up until the last 1% is correct? How much is perfectionism a part of your life?

You have been conditioned to be afraid that you may not be accepted and approved unless everything is perfect; in addition, you may also have been rewarded for paying attention to detail so you associate perfection with affirmation. You are being the proverbial good little boy or girl, striving to please so as to ward off criticism. Most people have an inner critic who keeps up a constant commentary, and at some stage we all manage to either silence or suppress this little person. If yours is alive and well (and in fact has a twin!), you are more critical of yourself than anyone else could ever be. If this rings true for you, then fear of not being perfect is a huge influence on your life.

| **No, this is not me** | **Yes, this is me** |
| --- | --- |

2. Are you afraid that there is not enough of you to go around? Do you have a constant feeling that others intrude into your space too much? Do you have to retreat away from people to a quiet place to rebalance? How much do you look at a request for action through the lens of whether you have the capacity to deliver it, rather than the need to just do it? This perspective can be described as operating from a *scarcity* viewpoint, where in certain circumstances you genuinely don't think that you have the resources to deal with the demands life, career or people make on you. You need to query how much your personal scarcity viewpoint influences what you do and how much or how little you get involved in. Could it be a hidden brake to developing the brand you want?

Opportunities can be presented to you, but you shy away from them, which can look like lack of ambition or, worse, laziness. It clearly isn't, but few people truly understand the fears associated with the scarcity perspective.

| **No, this is not me** | **Yes, this is me** |
| --- | --- |

3. Do you always prepare for the worst while hoping for the best? Do you habitually think of all the things that could go wrong and then organise your life to deal with them? Do you feel that you have only yourself to depend on? If you feel that, while you are safe-guarding the company, others around you are not seeing the difficulties that are obvious to you, is it possible that you may be overly problem-focused? The difficulty is that you may become trapped in a problem-focused space, and that can be easily misinterpreted by others as negativity or resistance to change. You know that it is not,

but the challenge is that constantly looking to safeguard against real or imagined problems can distort your perceptions and consequently your behaviour.

I have seen people fail to sign an important contract on behalf of a company because they wanted to ensure all safeguards were included. This became a moot point, however, when the deal failed because the contract was unacceptably delayed.

| No, this is not me | Yes, this is me |
|---|---|

### Do you like having lots of options?

Do you live in your head in a rich and wonderful world full of ideas and plans? Do you always look for options? Do you have difficulty tying yourself down as you wonder what is around the next corner? Do you get bored easily and always look for something new to distract you? If you are a great starter of projects but not a good finisher, you will end up in great difficulty in work as the details-orientated people will find you very frustrating.

If you are put in charge of something, do you find that you are really great at raising everyone's spirits and motivating them, but towards the end when it is getting routine or there is an intractable problem, do you have the tendency to disappear off into something more interesting, even if it is off the point?

The downside of this looking for new distractions is the difficulty in concentrating on the mundane details of the job. Every job has some mind-numbingly boring parts to it; even opera singers have to practice, sometimes for hours at a time. Ignoring the crucial basics is a bad career move; they are the foundation of every successful job. Often you can be caught out on the simplest of undone details, like not entering a vital piece of information into a database.

On the plus side, I have seen people who have the reputation of always coming up with new ideas in brainstorming meetings really succeed at the initial phases of a project. Indeed, they are also called on at problem stages when people become stalled as something is not working. They are lauded for this ability to ask lots of intriguing questions leading to new ideas and their personal brand receives a huge boost.

| No, this is not me | Yes, this is me |
|---|---|

### Do you need to express strong feelings?

Do you usually see to the heart of the problem and then just tell people what to do? Do you feel that the need to put people straight overrules everything else? Are you driven by a real sense of doing the right thing, saying the right thing and making it right?

You know the other person is wrong, and you like to tell it as it is, so you do, and then you cannot understand why they have a problem with your honesty. You tell everyone that you are a plain speaker and it's difficult to see why they have difficulty with that. You find the nuanced approach of some people to be manipulative, as it is not as honest as yours.

This need to be your authentic self in all circumstances causes problems for people in the corporate world where so much communication is indirect and where egos abound. You run the risk of upsetting all around you and getting a reputation of being difficult as you seem not to be able to get on with anyone.

Recognise this? Do you think that at heart you are a kind person, but somehow you end up upsetting everyone around you with your direct approach? Have you tried to change or do you dismiss behaving differently as being fake? I have seen people gravely damage their careers by insisting on plain speaking, even when it is clearly stopping their progress.

The downside of this directness is that often you fail to get people's willing cooperation, instead of just compliance to your authority. You may have had complaints about your communication style or, at worst, accusations of bullying behaviour.

| **No, this is not me** | **Yes, this is me** |
| --- | --- |

### Do you like to see others' points of view?

Do you easily see the situation from the perspective of others and identify with their stand? Do you sometimes get so immersed that you cannot get your own view across? This tendency to blend in can make you invisible to those around you and particularly to the more senior people who have a big say in your career progression. You may have been overlooked and are looking to blame someone, when the problem is that you are not doing anything to stand out.

Do you really like harmony and try to avoid conflict, even sublimating your own wishes? Take a really good look at yourself and decide how many times in the past month you acceded to the wishes of others even when you did not agree with the proposed action. How many times have you gone along just to keep the peace? Contrast this to the number of times you stood your ground and refused to budge. If the balance is all one way, you should be able to see that this form of harmony-seeking is a real driver of your behaviour.

Do you exert your own form of control by agreeing with the wishes of the most dominant person, but then quietly get your own way by not doing what they asked? Sometimes this is the only way harmony-seekers get to exert control. They agree to do something, especially when put under personal pressure, but then quietly retreat and decide not to do it. This can appear as incompetence, or I sometimes hear the word 'lazy' applied to a person displaying this behaviour.

Possibly the worst work situation for a harmony-seeker is to end up working for a dominant plain speaker. If you are in this situation, you may notice that you have begun to lose your energy and zest. You may lose the battle to exert your will at all, and you may become slowly overwhelmed.

| **No, this is not me** | Yes, this is me |
| --- | --- |

## What is my prime motivator?

You have now considered a number of possible motivators and one of them will probably have resonated quite strongly with you. To recap, have another brief look at each motivator and then rank them from one to 10 in order of how strongly you identified with them. Fill in the chart below. Look more closely at the top three, and then pick the one that is most like you, then pause and reflect on any way you see this motivator affecting your personal brand.

When you read Step 5 on brand drivers and derailers, you will get a chance to see if this motivator is in any way a threat to your personal brand.

## DECIDE ON YOUR PRIME MOTIVATOR

| Decide which of these is fundamental to you | Scale 1 to 10 | How is this affecting your personal brand? |
|---|---|---|
| 1. How much do you seek the approval of people around you by being helpful to them? | | |
| 2. How much does approval for your work and your results matter to you? | | |
| 3. When you meet someone or enter a new situation, do you immediately compare yourself to the others to see if you are good enough? | | |
| 4. Are you trying too hard and chasing perfection so as not to fail? | | |
| 5. Are you afraid that there is not enough of you to go around? | | |
| 6. Do you always prepare for the worst while hoping for the best? | | |
| 7. Do you like having lots of options? | | |
| 8. Are you very comfortable with expressing strong feelings? | | |
| 9. Do you find it easy to see other people's points of view? | | |

### Self-discovery: level 3 – the three selves

An important part of the self-discovery process is asking yourself: "How do the 'Three Selves In Me' – self-confidence, self-reliance and self-control – shape others' perception of me?"

### How self-confident are you?

On your own, quietly ask yourself: how confident do you feel? To help answer this, think about exactly how happy you are with yourself and how kind you are to yourself. Do you like yourself and what you have achieved? If you have a good view of yourself and like yourself, then you have strength and can build on it. It is at the core of self-confidence.

If you realise that you are not happy with yourself, reflect on the words you use to describe yourself. Are they harsh? Would you use them about anyone else? I frequently hear people describe themselves as 'lazy', 'unambitious', 'slow', 'awkward', 'withdrawn', 'boring', 'not a good socialiser'. Watch out for this, as negative self-talk can be a vicious self-fulfilling cycle. If you put yourself down, you feel down, you blame yourself, then put yourself down again, feel bad, and blame yourself. Around and around it goes. If you worry too much about what others think of you, if you have little trust in your own capabilities, if you don't think you can influence other people, then you can erode your own confidence.

Do you recognise any of this in yourself? If so, think how others may glimpse your lack of confidence? If you do not like yourself, will others? I recommend that you have a good look at the Johari exercise in the next step, as it gives you a structured way to allow others to tell you the good things about yourself. I have written about many confidence-boosting techniques in my book, *Shoeisms* (Morgan James, 2009). Have a look at them also.

## How self-reliant are you?

Have you thought about how self-reliant you are? Do you consider how much you direct your own actions? How much of an independent thinker are you? How much do you let other people's agendas control your actions?

If you have high self-reliance you will operate mostly from personal conviction and not from the need to meet others' demands. Low self-reliance sees you failing to take personal responsibility for crafting your own life.

A good example is when you are preparing a talk or presentation. With low self-reliance, you are afraid of what you will say; a self-reliant person will realise that they always know what to say. You are less likely to panic about a deadline, as you have confidence that you always meet these. You don't need to rely on others; you believe you can rely on yourself and your capabilities. A great way to build your confidence in your ability to cope is to begin a journal and each evening record situations where you took control, or solved a problem, or even where you were delighted that you survived and got through. Examples include dealing with a difficult colleague, handling a demanding customer and controlling your temper when provoked.

## How much self-control do you have?

Realising how much self-control you have may be harder than you think, so let's describe someone with low levels and benchmark off that.

Someone with low self-control hears or sees something that upsets them and they react straight away. They become emotional, dramatic and see themselves as a victim. They do not pause, think, consider, reflect, or see the other side before accessing their emotions. They are driven by their emotions and are highly reactive. It's often called the "amygdala hijack", a term coined by Daniel Goleman in his 1996 book, *Emotional Intelligence: Why It Can Matter More Than IQ*. It is an emotional response that is immediate and overwhelming and out of proportion to the actual stimulus, because the emotion has bypassed thinking completely.

You can imagine the opposite, a person who exudes calm under pressure. They think before they act. They look for causes, they have the ability to reframe situations and see others' views. I find myself constantly reframing situations for clients when they find themselves in victim mode because of an amygdala hijack. That reframing means having to really think about why a person says something, what is on their mind, their possible worries or fears, their previous behaviour. It allows them to pause and get the gift of perspective. I facilitate them to see what it would be like if they exercised more self-control.

I often recommend my clients to read a great book by the Arbinger Institute, *Leadership and Self-Deception: Getting Out of the Box* (2010), which clearly explains, with a story, how you can be someone with low self-control and therefore act the victim. It's a gem of a book, with many instructive insights. One of the most interesting is what they call "being in the box", that is, when you paint another person as the aggressor in order to perpetuate your role of victim.

### The triad of low self-confidence, low self-reliance and low self-control

There is an observable phenomenon that occurs when these three traits are all low in a person; they seem to affect and perpetuate each other. Imagine someone with low self-confidence who is not happy with themselves, does not trust their own judgement and overreacts when crossed: the *triad*. They can come across as a very troubled and difficult person. In my experience you come across one of these in most workplaces. The key question for you is, are you that person?

## How to pull all the insights together

You have now taken a good look at a number of aspects of yourself and are probably wondering what to do next. I recommend that you record all your conclusions on the checklist below, which allows you to take an overview of all your personal insights discussed above. It gives you a succinct overview all on one chart.

### THE SELF-DISCOVERY PROCESS: A CHECKLIST

| | Yes/No? | Do you see this as a strength or a weakness? |
|---|---|---|
| **Level 1: Outlook** | | |
| Are you mostly a positive person? | | |
| Are you mostly a pessimist? | | |
| Do you let bad news affect all aspects of your life? | | |
| **Level 2: Prime Motivator** | | |
| Are you looking for approval by helping people? | | |
| Are you looking for approval by working to impress? | | |
| Are you looking for approval every time you meet someone? | | |
| Is fear ruling your life, through chasing perfection? | | |
| Is fear ruling your life because you don't think there is enough of you for everyone? | | |
| Is fear ruling your life, so you prepare for the worst? | | |
| Do you like having lots of options? | | |
| Are you comfortable with expressing strong feelings? | | |
| Do you find it easy to see other people's points of view? | | |
| **Level 3: The Three Selves** | | |
| How self-confident are you? | | |
| How self-reliant are you? | | |
| How much self-control do you have? | | |

At this stage I would like you to begin the process of deciding on the implications of the discoveries you have made.

## The implications of your discoveries

Divide your answers into strengths and weaknesses and thoughtfully consider the implications for your personal brand. It is important to note these now before you go on to looking at your success to date.

| Strengths | What are the implications for my personal brand? |
|---|---|
| 1. | |
| 2. | |
| 3. | |
| 4. | |
| 5. | |
| 6. | |
| 7. | |

| Weaknesses | What are the implications for my personal brand? |
|---|---|
| 1. | |
| 2. | |
| 3. | |
| 4. | |
| 5. | |
| 6. | |
| 7. | |

This record of your findings is a significant enhancement of your self-understanding and the beginning of you realising how knowing yourself is a foundation of your personal brand. Here's an example of how someone did these exercises and found that a real weakness was ruining her personal brand.

## SOPHIA: KNOWING YOUR PRIME MOTIVATOR CAN
## TRANSFORM YOUR APPROACH

Sophia worked in administration and operations in a not-for-profit organisation. She was well regarded because of her hard work and attention to detail. She was a bit of a workhorse and so, in her office's culture of overworking, she was valued and relied on. Yet despite this her career had paused. She came to me as she knew she was doing all the right things, yet the rewards were not coming in terms of promotion and interesting new work.

Sophia did a good deal of self-exploration using personality tests; she observed her behaviours under different circumstances and finally we found what was holding her back. She discovered that:
- she was mostly negative, mostly pessimistic and she let her unhappiness in work affect her whole life;
- her prime motivator was fear;
- she was not self-confident, had low self-reliance and medium self-control.

Sophia always took the negative view, and she was motivated by the fear that her pessimistic view would come true. This served her well in the early stages of her career because she watched everything. A fly did not land in her department but she knew about it. Her immediate boss loved her, he could relax, he was protected. When he left he was replaced by someone more ambitious who wanted to be seen to be involved in new initiatives, solving problems with innovative approaches. When he arrived he asked Sophia for ideas, but she did not know how to think about scary innovations. She viewed her new boss's suggestions as risky; she found 101 problems in all his proposals. She may have been right some of the time, but her overwhelming fear was misinterpreted as stubborn non-cooperation and resistance to change. It was not. Sophia wanted the best for the organisation she loved, but she could not help but see the dangers in all these new suggestions.

Sophia's new boss neither understood her caution nor valued her perspective; she simply did not fit his purpose of reforming the operations. So her career stalled. Worse, her boss began to damage her brand by characterising her as difficult and resistant to changing and going in a new direction.

Sophia took a while to realise that her fear and concern to protect against the unforeseen had worked in better times, but in lean times innovation was needed. Something had to change and some work practices needed to be drastically altered. Of course, there were dangers, but they were outweighed by the risk of not changing. She was so paralysed by the fear that this fast change of pace caused her that she went into an overwhelmed state.

She knew she had to change, but that's easier said than done, so she worked on observing and recording her challenges on a daily basis. She worked really hard on accurate self-observation of how she viewed each challenge, and how much negativity, pessimism and fear and the need to protect figured in her perception of the situation. Sophia realised that it played a larger part than she knew. That piece of self-knowledge was pivotal in changing her.

Fear still played a part, but she was aware of it now and was able to control it and keep it in perspective. She worked on the pessimism and fought to control her reactions. As she began to see things more positively, her pessimism receded, as did her fear. Not surprisingly, as she gave herself the chance to shine, her self-confidence rose.

Sophia had to work hard to change her boss's opinion of her, but as she did he began to see her as a questioner and protector of the organisation rather than intrinsically negative and so he began to realise that she was a net contributor to the organisation.

The issues you've raised and observed here will be addressed in the following steps, where we will explore how behaviours shape a personal brand. Now you need to move on to the next phase of exploring your strengths and finding your successes by completing the self-discovery process in looking around you and augmenting your internal inquiry with the insights of others.

# Step 2

## Build self-knowledge: look around you

*"We are the veils that veil us from ourselves."*

R.D. Laing

® **Your personal strengths and successes**
® **Your personal brand statement**

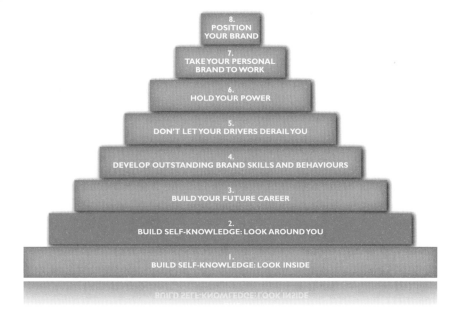

## Your personal strengths and successes

Now that you have looked at yourself and discovered many things, you need to go to others and, in a disciplined way, discover the other dimensions to you. No matter how honest we are with ourselves and how much we continuously reflect on our makeup, we still need the reality check of others' perceptions of us. It provides food for thought. You may discover, as many of my clients do, that you have been too hard on yourself and that you are held in high esteem by many people. I firmly believe that we are hard enough on ourselves without inviting any more negative comments, which is why I recommend asking people to tell you what is good about you, what about you impresses them, not what challenges you may have.

## What do others think you are good at?

With the insights into yourself gained from Step 1, you now need to move to another level where you begin to look around you at the impact you have had in your career to date, and to concentrate on noting the unique attributes and skills other people see in you, to add to the self-knowledge you have just gathered. You will also get valuable insights from key people. This goes to the heart of how people describe you when you leave the room.

### The Johari Window

To help enhance your understanding, you can discover what others think using a version of the Johari window exercise. Based on a technique developed by Joseph Luft and Harrington Ingham in the 1950s ('Jo' and 'Hari'), it is a wonderfully simple way to get a sense of how you are perceived by others. The figure below sets out the concept.

There are two views of 'you': yours and other people's and they intersect in four ways:

| | Other people's view of you | |
|---|---|---|
| **Your view of you** | **A** Open area: known to you and outsiders | **C** Blind area: known only to outsiders |
| | **B** Hidden area: known only to you | **D** Unknown area to you and outsiders |

The aim of the exercise is to discover the perceptions of others that are unknown to you: quadrant C. We are only looking for positive feedback in order to give you strong building blocks for a remarkable personal brand; we are not interested in any negative feedback or opinions. This may look like a contradiction here, seeking out what other people think but limiting it to positive feedback only, but I want you to receive only positive and encouraging insights as they are **more useful**. It is all too easy for people to be negative in giving insights, but more meaningful when they have to reflect and find positive things to say.

## Who, what, how: rules to carry out the Johari Window exercise

**Who should you ask?**
- Only ask **positive** people (you have enough of your own negative thoughts).
- Ask people you **admire** and whose opinion you know will be well thought out (why ask someone you don't rate to give you feedback?).
- Ask people who **care about you** and mean you well (why invite negative, hurtful people into your inner space?).
- Ask people you **trust**.

Remember you are dealing with your career here, so try to get people who know you in a business setting. Often people ask their partner, and while that can be useful I suggest you be braver and ask colleagues, customers and others in a work setting.

**What do you ask?**    Tell them you are undertaking an exercise as part of your career development. You are doing an audit of your assets – the biggest one being you. You want to use their insights to build a personal brand.

Specifically say: "I am planning my career and I need your help. I am looking to find out a unique attribute that I have to use in developing my personal brand. When I know this, it will help me to move to the next level in my career."

You are looking for the golden nugget, an insight that will greatly encourage you.

**How do you approach it?**    Be very business-like about this and choose your person carefully. Thoroughly explain the exercise and give them a written request. Ask them to give you a written reply. Some people may want to help you but can find it difficult to find the starting point, so you can help them by prompting them with a list of adjectives. You could circle the ones you agree with for yourself and provide a fresh list to them – this is a good starting point.

Give them a few days to do it, no more. Ask for the returned document on a specific day. This way you have set them up to do it seriously, and believe me, if you do this set-up correctly you will get serious and insightful replies.

**What are the results?**   I have used this exercise with clients and found it profoundly affected their levels of confidence. The feedback works on many levels. At a basic level, it is affecting to realise that you are well regarded, even admired. At another it is a gift to have your impact articulated positively by people you admire. Do not underestimate the power this has to build your self-confidence.

Finally, you get a view of the impact of the self you project into the world. This may be a first for you. You glimpse that elusive space, the aspects of your projection that people are picking up on and what they really value. The more insightful and clever the people you ask, the more penetrating the observations. You see now why asking bright, positive and well-intentioned people is so vital.

| Name | Key comments |
| --- | --- |
| 1. | |
| 2. | |
| 3. | |
| 4. | |
| 5. | |
| 6. | |
| 7. | |
| 8. | |
| 9. | |
| 10. | |

Have a really good look at the comments and extract the most frequent ones. They are all valuable, but one that is named by a number of people is clearly indicating a *signature* strength. That will be a key part of your personal brand, based on the authentic you.

**Signature strengths mentioned by more than one person**

1.

2.

3.

4.

5.

**Signature strengths identified by you**

1.

2.

3.

4.

5.

This would be a good time to add on the signature strengths you have identified in Step 1.

## Combine your strengths with your successes

I recommend that you start by examining your career to date and focusing on examples of where you thought you did very well, instances where you felt you impressed and delivered something notable. Be kind to yourself here and realise that something you may have thought normal may have been exceptional in the eyes of others. List them in the table overleaf.

| What are my successes in my career to date? | What did I do to make it a success? | What signature strength does it cross-reference with? |
|---|---|---|
| 1. | | |
| 2. | | |
| 3. | | |
| 4. | | |
| 5. | | |
| 6. | | |
| 7. | | |
| 8. | | |
| 9. | | |
| 10. | | |

That is a very realistic starting point for planning a personal brand. Use this chart as a guide when you bring all your work together. Having a realistic view of yourself, you can now begin the process of crafting a personal brand statement.

## ANNETTE AND DONAL: THE EFFECT OF JOHARI INSIGHTS ON PERSONAL BRAND

### Annette

Imagine the difference to Annette to be told by nine separate business colleagues from across a career of 20 years that she had the unique ability to mould trusting and long-lasting business relationships and to sustain them, even amid disagreements. She knew she could build relationships, but she did not know it was seen as a distinct attribute of hers or how widely valued a quality it was. This propelled her to aspire to seek a position at the highest levels of business, where deals are done personally and relationships are key.

### Donal

Donal was just starting in a new consultancy and had lost some of his confidence after the initial months; he began to doubt he was good enough for the company. The Johari feedback he received from previous clients was a gift as he started to make his name in the new consultancy. He was working to convince the partners he had been worth hiring. His feedback told him that his razor-sharp analytical skills, coupled with deft aptitude for making complex issues understandable, topped with his frankness, was seen by previous clients as of incalculable value. Even if he might have made them uncomfortable occasionally, he had made them richer.

Working with this insightful positive feedback, when Donal met future potential clients he knew he was of value, that he could change their understanding of their business to allow them to make necessary changes. They responded to that inner confidence and he landed more business.

## Up your game

When people start thinking about the words they would like to be used to describe them they start at a low level and say things like:

- Dependable
- Efficient
- Hard worker
- Agreeable
- Friendly
- Nice
- Good time-keeper
- Good team player
- Loyal.

Let's face it, these are really only entry-level words. You need all of these to even get in the door. What we are looking for are inspiring words and phrases, like these:

- Creative
- One to watch
- Can be relied on to deliver beyond expectations
- The one who makes change happen
- An energiser
- A great deal-maker
- An innovator.

## Your personal brand statement

### I. Strengths and successes

Reflect on all the insights you have gained and summarise below the insights that you feel are most useful to you.

| My personal brand relies on these strengths | I know I am successful when I ... |
|---|---|
| I. | I. |
| 2. | 2. |
| 3. | 3. |
| 4. | 4. |
| 5. | 5. |
| 6. | 6. |
| 7. | 7. |
| 8. | 8. |
| 9. | 9. |
| 10. | 10. |

### 2. What do you want to be known as?

Identify what you would like to stand for and what you would like to project, based on a clear understanding of your strengths, particularly your signature ones, backed up by your assessment of when and how you were successful. This is a firm foundation to start crafting your personal brand.

Let's start with declaring what you want to be known as. Examples include:
- The person who always leads our successful company acquisitions
- The person who delivers the biggest client accounts
- The go-to person on negotiation in the company
- The likely new director
- The next partner
- The most innovative person
- A real problem-solver.

Now decide and record what you would like to be known as and what your personal brand will be.

| My personal brand will be: |
| --- |
| 1. |
| 2. |
| 3. |
| 4. |
| 5. |
| 6. |
| 7. |
| 8. |
| 9. |
| 10. |

You now have a good idea of yourself and what others think of you. Next, you need to look at your career and your plans for the future. When you have done that, you will be in an excellent position to combine this with the results of the previous step and begin building the personal brand you want.

## ANTHONY: COASTING IN A COMFORT ZONE

Anthony worked for a professional business organisation for 15 years. He was in the number two spot for about seven years, having been promoted there in slow-but-steady stages. He was good at his job, well liked and very easy to work with. He thought everything was going well and that he was progressing steadily in his career.

Disruption to his comfort zone came from an unexpected quarter when, unexpectedly, his boss applied for and received a sabbatical to work at a sister organisation in another country. Change was foisted onto Anthony. In truth, he had been mildly unfulfilled for about three years, especially as he was now 40 and his family were hinting that he might have more potential than he was showing.

Anthony was offered the position of Acting CEO for the year. It was one thing for Anthony to be a happy but disgruntled person, but another to have to suddenly decide whether or not he wanted to step into his boss's shoes.

Largely pushed into it by people who saw his latent ability, Anthony took the position and began his year of acting up. He was amazed at how much he enjoyed being the boss and how good he was at it. He saw how much vainglorious mystique the absent boss had woven into the role. He realised he was just as good as his predecessor, and actually had some really good new ideas.

That year, Anthony carried out the role of spokesperson, appearing on TV and radio programmes, opening and closing conferences and generally being really good at the job.

As with all good things, it came to an end. The boss came back and everyone readjusted to the pre-sabbatical situation. At least on the surface they did, but what no one could have predicted was that Anthony, like the genie, had tasted power and freedom and was not happy to be put back into the bottle.

That is when I met Anthony and began working with him. Until that time, he had never questioned himself or really thought at all about his abilities or ambitions. He realised just how much he had drifted through his thirties.

Spurred on by his determination not to drift again, Anthony began to explore in some detail what was happening in his career and what he could do to take more control. We started with his exploration of his personal brand. Quickly we realised that his biggest challenge was his complete lack of self-knowledge.

Many people slip into easy jobs in companies early in their careers and stay in the one company passively progressing up the ranks without much effort or planning. They don't go for interviews or test themselves against outsiders, instead they just morph as the organisation demands. In many instances, the organisation itself doesn't really change; it just grows into a bigger version of itself. So there's no big challenge and no impetus to stop and examine oneself. Look around you. Companies are full of people like this who have never had to really examine their skills or career plans. The collapse of big organisations like banks, building societies and large retailers has rocked many complacent people into self-examination.

So Anthony began to look at himself, and using many personality tests and exercises he began to get insights into how he perceived the world, how he made sense of it, his motivations, his drivers and his default behaviours. He realised that he was a lover of harmony; he avoided conflict completely, to the extent of sitting on his own ambitions if he thought they would cause bother.

Anthony had chosen to coast along, as it was the easiest thing to do. The only reason he changed was because circumstances and advocates had cleared the path for him. He became aware of his inertia and how much it ran his life. He realised he had a perfection-ist streak, so he was not going to risk change unless he could con-trol the process and do it in his way, to his standards. He saw how a change-averse perfectionist could end up in the same place for 20 years and not see the time go by.

To bolster his self-exploration in a constructive way, I got Anthony to do the Johari Exercise and ask trusted and positive colleagues to tell him something about his unique attributes and skills. It was a revelation for him. He saw that others really appreciated his tal-ents. They highlighted his quiet but strong leadership, his coopera-tive approach, his ability to develop relationships, his optimism and his long experience. A really encouraging insight was the number of people who considered that he had the potential to work at a higher level and contribute to the leadership of the organisation. Anthony also learned that a lot of his colleagues had wondered why he was not more ambitious, as he was undoubtedly talented.

Anthony would tell you today that he was stunned by the discov-eries he made about himself. I remember well the day he came and said that, over the weekend, he was unable to sleep as he was thinking so much. All his self-discovery work made him realise that he was sleepwalking through his career and that he had talent, but that time was finite.

The genie was now well and truly out of the bottle. Because he was aware of himself and could work to leverage his strengths, Anthony went looking for a new position somewhere else and got a CEO position in a new company where they were delighted to have him.

At this stage you have the benefit of having looked at yourself in the self-discovery process; in addition, you now have the perspective of others. You can develop a more rounded view of your personal brand as you reflect on where the two views may match or differ.

I have seen people who wanted to believe that they were skilled at something and then be delighted and very encouraged when the comments came to them from the exercise confirming that they were not only good at this skill, but in fact it was a signature strength of theirs. Seeking the positive input of others allows you to either confirm a hoped-for strength or let you see something others believe you are brilliant at, but that is hidden to you.

# Step 3

## Build your future career

*"The secret of achievement is to hold a picture of a successful outcome in the mind."*

Henry David Thoreau

® **Your present career and your plan**
® **The implications of a Big Audacious Aim for your personal brand**
® **Develop your Big Audacious Aim**

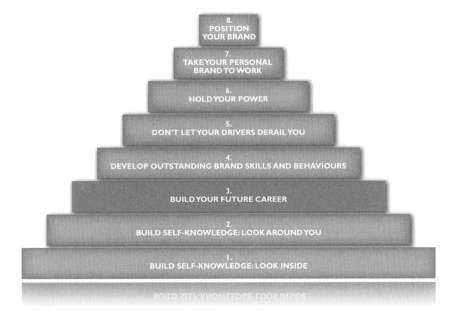

## Your present career and your plan

The previous step gave you the insights and tools to increase your knowledge of your own personality – the centrepiece of your personal brand. Now you need to move to the next phase in building your brand. You must explore your career aspirations and plans and how they connect to your personal brand.

The connection between your career and your personal brand is so strong that you should think of them as being intertwined so that you are not wasting effort building a personal brand in a career vacuum. At the same time, you are failing if you try to build a career without simultaneously building a personal brand.

Your plan for the future and the present stage in your career are the backdrop to the development of your personal brand. Because we are talking about your personal brand in a career context, it makes perfect sense to take time and see if you're working to a career plan or not.

## Your Big Audacious Aim

I would like to introduce you to my career-planning concept, the 'Big Audacious Aim', or the BAA for short, to describe where you are aiming for in your career. I usually recommend that you take a five-year perspective and consider where you want to be at that time. The word 'audacious' is significant. It is meant to suggest to you something requiring courage and to distinguish it from a less ambitious goal. A goal is something you set with a time frame, for example: "I will develop and deliver that strategy by the first of June". A Big Audacious Aim is more ambitious, broader, more of a stretch for you. It takes time to develop and, when arrived at, will feel perfectly correct to you.

It might seem like a daunting task to develop a clear view of where you will be in your career in five years, but it is possible, and doing so can transform your outlook.

The best way to start this new thinking process is to answer the following questions:
- What work do I enjoy the most? What is my passion?
- What am I significantly the best at? (It is always best to play to your strengths.)
- What can I make money at? I am all for being fulfilled, but also realistic enough to know money is a vital part of the average person's career. Mine anyway!
- Is this Big Audacious Aim a little bit challenging, even frightening? (Remember it is an audacious aim, not a comfortable goal.)

### Ask why you want to do something

As you ponder options for your Big Audacious Aim, it helps to ask *why* you want to do something, because then *how* you do it comes more easily.

Many of us blindly follow a career path and don't stop to really review why we have chosen to build our careers in a particular area. I frequently work with people at a stage in their career where they realise that they no longer want to work in their present company, or they want to completely change professions, or want to escape a full-time job and begin to experiment with a portfolio of options. They are at a crossroads and have suddenly begun asking themselves why they are doing something they no longer enjoy.

It's revealing to examine the reasons we do things. When we do them because we have to, our motivation is reduced; if we do them out of joy, our motivation abounds. Sadly, many young people choose careers because of external influences and so are not intrinsically motivated:

- Tradition ("Our family are all doctors" or "It's a family business; all the sons work in it").
- "I was told that there were jobs in this area and now there aren't, so I have to emigrate."
- "I like people so I went into hotel management, now I hate the job because it's all about dealing with people and their unreasonable demands."
- "Accountants are never out of work, it's a good profession."
- "All my class applied to that consultancy firm, it's very prestigious."

Focus on the *why*. Choosing an endeavour that you like, are interested in, that excites you and that allows you freedom and flexibility, will make it easier to achieve.

## Futurists and minute-to-minute people

When I ask people to do this exercise they divide immediately into two groups: the first group comprises those who have a very future-centred approach and have no difficulty seeing themselves in five or even 10 years' time. They naturally have a big vision view of the world. If you are one of these, start right away and answer the questions.

If you are in the other camp and cannot easily see the future in this way, but move from minute-to-minute, day-to-day, then I have another tool to help you. It is called a 'vision board'. Get a notice board in a stationery shop and pin it to the wall. You can also use online tools like Pinterest. Then begin to look for images of what you like to pin on your board: places you would like to work, cities you want to work in, activities you are interested in, a course you want to study, role models you would like to emulate, journals or blogs you would like to write for, conferences at which you would like to present, etc. Look for images that ignite your imagination. The mind thinks in pictures, so this is a way to kick-start your imagination.

## Imaginings

As you build the vision board and the images begin to fill the surface, you will begin to see the patterns. It makes a great jumping-off point for discussion. Remember one of Einstein's most famous sayings and let it guide you: "Imagination is more important than knowledge".

Creating a vision board will leave you much better placed to construct your Big Audacious Aim. The real advantage to you of having a BAA is that you can map out a trajectory over a number of years to reach it. It gives you a firm outcome to aim for, but does not tie you too rigidly to the process of getting there.

Is it only me, or are you noticing how time seems to fly by and one birthday merges into the next? Many audience members in the talks I give say the same. So if time is vanishing, ask yourself: Do I have a long-term (five-year) view of my career, or will I wake up tomorrow and find another five years have passed? Here is a test for you: can you remember what you did for your birthday five years ago? See how five years can vanish into the fog. Just think: five years can vanish and you may wake up in the same job, in the same company and not have developed your career at all. You don't necessarily need to change jobs to develop if you are constantly pushing and developing yourself.

## Having a Big Audacious Aim really works

I have known people who have mapped out a career path to being a thought leader in their speciality and undertake a change of career and do postgraduate degrees; women who combine pregnancy, childbirth and maternity leave with a master's degree in order to reach their Big Audacious Aim. They find the ability and motivation to do this by accessing a state of 'flow' in their work.

The concept of being in a state of 'flow' is important when you are deciding how you want to direct your career. Being in 'flow' is where you excel because you are doing what you love, are deeply involved and committed. Artists frequently achieve this state. I have introduced this concept to my clients and they have found it remarkably useful. When you know how to recognise the work and the circumstances that bring it about, you can try to bring about this state for yourself. Once you do this, once you notice an increase in energy, motivation, imagination and creative force, you begin to love being in a state of flow.

It is an uplifting ambition to try to experience this in your career. I encourage you to bring it about in your work. Remember, everything you want is on the other side of fear, so be brave in envisioning a future for yourself. If you don't have courage and belief in yourself, who will?

## Develop your Big Audacious Aim

In writing down your BAA, don't write it in the future tense as if you merely aim to achieve it. I recommend that you write it in the present tense, as if you have already achieved it; this is more powerful. It is also a good idea to include some emotion, with phrases like 'I am enjoying being or doing ...'. ('I am enjoying being a director earning €150,000 a year.') Finally, put a date on it to make it crystal clear.

It should look like this:

---

**Big Audacious Aim**

I am enjoying ...

.......................................................................................

.......................................................................................

.......................................................................................

.......................................................................................

On   .............................

    (day/month/year)

---

### Milestones to your Big Audacious Aim

To make your Big Audacious Aim more real in the immediate future, I suggest deciding on milestones to define progress and to give you motivating short-term outcomes.

### ANDREA: A STORY ABOUT SETTING MILESTONES

Andrea came to me to work on her career plan. She was a senior executive in a large national company but felt strongly that she was stalling and losing interest in her job. To an outside observer she appeared dynamic, ambitious and focused, but in reality she was faking it, as she felt quite dispirited. Her boss would have been stunned to hear that she was so fed-up she was thinking of quitting, even though she did not have another job to go to.

Though she was one of the most capable women I have ever met and had mastered her brief, she was now beginning to feel bored; she could see no new challenges where she was.

Andrea worked on her Big Audacious Aim and announced to me that she would like to be the CEO of a medium-sized company and then to set up and grow her own significant company. That was a worthy Big Audacious Aim. The thought of it electrified her; you could see the transformation as it was both engaging and frightening – the ideal ingredients of a good Big Audacious Aim. Why? The answer is that you need to give an active, adventurous mind something to wrestle with or it will become bored and sometimes self-destructive.

Now come the milestones. The first question for Andrea was: would it help realise her Big Audacious Aim if she left her current job, or could she turn this around by making it part of her journey?

First, she drew up the five annual milestones, what she would achieve at the end of each of the next five years. Then she added intermediate half-year mini-milestones. This is what it looked like:

| Year | Mini Milestone: After Six Months | Annual Milestone: After 12 Months |
|---|---|---|
| 1 | Do the Institute of Directors' Chartered Directors qualification. <br><br> Get directorship of allied company to build business knowledge. | Make significant contribution to board. |
| 2 | Get second directorship. <br><br> Become a speaker on my subject. | Have established reputation at board level. <br><br> Become a thought leader in my industry. |
| 3 | Move up or out to senior level, VP or Director. <br><br> Be nominated for awards. | Establish strong profile at board and VP level. <br><br> Become sought-after as go-to person in my field. |
| 4 | Have head-hunters queuing around block with the 'right' jobs. | Land the right CEO job. |
| 5 | Decide to stay and grow company or begin own company. | Have doubled salary, become thought leader, serving on boards. |

The idea is to give yourself a series of stepped accomplishments to guide you. Now consider how Andrea's brand will intertwine with this plan:

- If she is to get a board directorship, she needs to look, speak, act and channel the brand of a successful board director.
- If she is to become an accomplished speaker, she needs to learn the best speaking skills and get lots of opportunities to hone those skills. She must learn stagecraft, look and act the part of a speaker. She can no longer run insignificant workshops as she builds the profile of thought leader.

Each step of the way demands a fine tune of her personal brand. It changes as her accomplishments build and her aspirations grow. The effect on Andrea of this process of building the Big Audacious Aim, milestones and congruent personal brand was astonishing. Her ambition was harnessed, her energy and intellect focused and her motivation rose as she married her aspirations with her job.

## Your present career

As you begin the process of developing your Big Audacious Aim and new career plan, look now at how you are behaving in your present job. Let's look at five issues:

1. The implications of a Big Audacious Aim for your personal brand.
2. Have you a proactive view of your career?
3. Are you a victim of 'keep the head down and they'll notice me' syndrome?
4. Are you proactively pushing your career in your present situation?
5. Do you have a mentor?

### 1. The implications of a Big Audacious Aim for your personal brand

Having a powerful personal Big Audacious Aim will motivate you. You will tend to be more focused in your career path, taking one step at a time, but in a directed way, always building on the last thing.

The opposite is true of a lot of people who suddenly realise that they are in the wrong job or they have begun to wander aimlessly in their career. They have stayed too long in one company and become comfortable or they have suffered in a company that does not value its employees.

In many instances, they have stagnated in their job and have lost confidence as a result. They lack motivation and direction, and frequently have a poor personal brand. They are seen as disillusioned, bored and switched off. Have you heard the phrase "rolling down to retirement"? It means that everyone knows that you will not take a risk or confront anyone in case it jeopardises your pension, or that you have your eyes fixed so firmly on the exit door that you are coasting along, doing the minimum, just waiting to get out.

## 2. Have you a proactive view of your career?

One of the most striking ways your career and brand connect is through your level of ambition. Ambition is usually accompanied by drive and energy and that appears in your personal brand. Energetic, driven people get the name of being 'go-getters'. It's a self-fulfilling prophecy. Imagine the mindset of a busy director: she needs a project delivered in three months, it involves sticky negotiations with difficult but powerful internal stakeholders – it must not fail. She looks around the floor and sees a bright, driven and ambitious person. Will he deliver on time, have the energy to stick it out, know how important it is, be grateful for the chance and know not to blow it? Yes. He gets the opportunity.

She picked up on his personal brand, which told her he was capable and ambitious. It's a bit of a 'chicken-and-egg' situation really: do you get the opportunities because you have built a go-getter brand or do you develop the brand because you got the opportunities? The important thing is that you get what you ask for and are ready for opportunities. Don't ask, don't get.

## 3. Are you a victim of 'keep the head down and they'll notice me' syndrome?

A cautionary word! I have seen a large number of women fall victim to the 'keep the head down and they will notice me' syndrome. I also call it the Good Girl/Boy Syndrome – the firm belief that if you stay at your desk and work hard, deliver results and add value, people will notice and you will be rewarded. Somehow the bossy executives will seek you out, literally walk all the way down to your desk, find you behind the potted plant, call you up on high and reward you for all your silent and uncomplaining diligence. Really? How much of this have you actually seen? Except in parts of the public service where the seniority rule applies and you eventually rise to the top if you work diligently enough and stay long enough. Most senior people ignore the head-downers. They get taken for granted, become resentful and blame other people's lack of concern. This is a bad strategy.

Drifting along in your career, ignoring your personal brand is ultimately self-destructive. Yet I see and hear it every day, most often from women. I make this point in every speech I give to women executives. I cannot bear to see women accepting this way of working. I have questioned many women on this and often they say that they find pushing yourself forward to be 'fake', and they reject it.

Again, you have a self-fulfilling prophecy. You have built a personal brand: a dull one; it is the quiet, unambitious, accepting, reactive, diligent workhorse. It is not the bright one: proactive, challenging, spirited, ambitious, driven, seeking, pushy and engaging. So the paradox is that as you work harder and stay later, silently delivering, you are being seen as the dull one, even though inside you believe you are the bright one. Beware the accidental brand!

If you are in this predicament, then you need to take a more proactive role in developing your own career. You need to build your personal brand and carry out all the steps in this book. Believe me, Good Girls or Boys do not get the corner office.

## 4. Are you proactively pushing your career in your present situation?

Are you proactively asking your boss what he is going to do to help you develop your career? Appraisals and end-of-year chats of all sorts should be a two-way process. Too many people miss that opportunity when they have the boss opposite them, focused on them, and they don't ask the all-important question for their career: "What plans have you in mind for me in the next year or two? What new things will I be doing? What new teams will I be involved in? What are my stretch goals?" This is a big part of your brand development as it shows that you have ambition and energy.

I recently advised Matthew, a young man, and a rising star in my opinion, as he was preparing for his annual appraisal with his boss. I introduced him to the concept of the 'Performance/Potential Matrix' (see overleaf). Use these parameters to ascertain where you are seen in this matrix: your performance in the job; and your potential to grow and develop in your career in the company. What 'box' are you in?

## PERFORMANCE/POTENTIAL MATRIX

| | Potential | | |
|---|---|---|---|
| **Performance** | High Performance Low Potential | High Performance Medium Potential | High Performance High Potential |
| | Medium Performance Low Potential | Medium Performance Medium Potential | Medium Performance High Potential |
| | Low Performance Low Potential | Low Performance Medium Potential | Low Performance High Potential |

## MATTHEW: BE PROACTIVE IN PROGRESSING YOUR CAREER

Matthew was an extremely hard-working person and very good at his job. He had a boss who was focused on her own career and who found him very useful, as he did more than his fair share of work, made zero mistakes and generally made her look good. He thought that she was delighted to have him in her team and really did not want to lose him, as she would be exposed and her job would be harder. That was a good insight on his part.

As Matthew described his situation, I suggested to him that he change his view of his boss and be more demanding of her. To my mind, she had put him in the High Performance but Low Potential box. And she had not thought about what she should do to develop a valued employee. She did not think of him as having a career trajectory or that she had any obligation to develop him. She liked him, appreciated his work, but that was it.

In the appraisal meeting Matthew raised these issues and asked her outright what she planned for him in developmental terms. She said she would need to think about it (decoded: she was very surprised and had no answer). Matthew's boss looked at the situation again, and he has since been given new responsibilities, more access to cross-functional teams and, I believe, a new-found respect.

At the next Christmas party, at the end of the night Matthew's boss confided that she had been shocked at his analysis and more than impressed at his challenging her. She felt he had called her on her obligations and she was grown-up enough to take it.

## 5. Do you have a mentor?

One of the most important things you can do for your career is to get yourself a mentor. If you can afford a programme with an experienced external mentor, then you will have ready access to a trusted and detached advisor who focuses on your career. If your company has a company mentor programme, join it tomorrow. If not, ask them why not and get one started. If you are a woman in a predominantly male company, ask for a programme to address any inequality issues and, if needed, ask for a development programme to increase the number of women progressing through the company to the top leadership level.

How you cope with challenges in work and how you handle your career progression are key ingredients of your brand, and having top-class advice from a mentor can only increase the impact of your personal brand. You can have more than one mentor, for different aspects of your career. If you cannot understand or deal with organisational politics, get a mentor who has already successfully navigated to the top. Their advice over a lunch could transform your career progression. If you feel you are not being noticed, or that you are being hemmed in by one difficult boss, you can seek advice from a mentor up the line or in a different company on how to navigate around the obstacle.

A mentor may advise you for a period of time, meeting every month or just once or twice on a particular issue. I recommend that once you have established a regular meeting schedule with a mentor, arrange a list of questions for each meeting, or e-mail them your challenges in advance for discussion.

The paradox I observe is that the best people openly embrace the concept of having a mentor, while the ones most in need of guidance usually refuse to try it. Really good people continue to get more and more external input into their careers and so they thrive. They build an alliance of advisors to help them through the challenges. The opposite is true of people who think they are above help or advice. I have seen first-hand the career suicide of people who are resistant to help and who believe that they are as they are and they have no need for objective input from others. The most frequent example of this is the person with painfully low levels of self-knowledge who simply cannot see the effect they are having on those around them. They have a bad personal brand that they nurture into a truly toxic one over a period of years. If you have had no one to discuss your career with, to get unbiased input from, to update you on your personal brand, then you need to address this.

At this stage you have a good sense of yourself and what others consider your strengths and you have thought about your future career and developed your Big Audacious Aim. You have built the foundations of a purposeful personal brand. You know who you are and where you are going.

The next step is to examine your skills and behaviours and how they will help or hinder your purposeful personal brand. If you don't do this, you will be proceeding in a blind fashion on two fronts: run the risk of not having the requisite skills to deliver your BAA, or have behaviours that damage your personal brand.

# Step 4

## Develop outstanding brand skills and behaviours

*"The secret of success is to do the common things uncommonly well."*
John D. Rockefeller

- ® **Impression points**
- ® **First impressions**
- ® **Communication skills**
- ® **Leadership skills**
- ® **Adding value to the company**

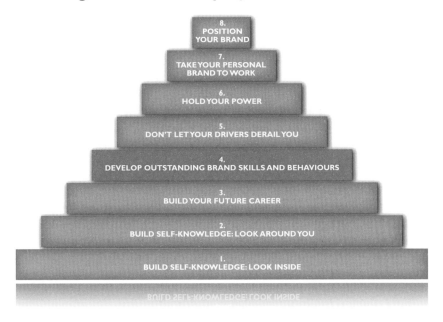

## Behaviours define your personal brand

A large part of your personal brand revolves around your skills and behaviours, and I would like to introduce you to this vital dimension. You may have heard the saying by Carl Jung: "You are what you do, not what you say you'll do."

Your behaviours define your personal brand. It is vital that you are aware of them and are not behaving unconsciously. I see lots of accidental bullies – people who are actually quite kind but who, in certain career positions and when frustrated and under pressure, exhibit all the bad behaviour of a bully. When confronted with the evidence of the damage they are causing, they are often shocked.

It's so easy to say you will change. A lot of people focus on small but instant changes to their behaviour. When you do this, all the big behavioural challenges pile up behind, unchanged. When you try to change everything you succeed for a day or two then revert to your default setting. It's easy to say yes to becoming an entirely different person. That's not what I want you to do: it will not work. Instead, I want you to focus and say yes to *specific*, meaningful changes.

Start by reading this step, then move to Step 5 on drivers and derailers, and then onto Step 6 on holding and leaking power. These three steps taken as a whole will give you a thorough guide to developing outstanding personal brand-building behaviours.

Every time you walk into a room you make an impression, every time you walk back out you leave that impression more lastingly on the people in the room. I am always surprised at how this obvious point is missed by so many people who concentrate only on their work and don't care about the package it is delivered in, namely themselves. Others can be so tuned-out of the need to make an impression that they have a 'take it or leave it' attitude; today in business I find too many people are leaving it.

I see executives every day who are ignoring their personal brand and who are struggling in their career. They don't know why, as they think they are working hard and delivering results. They treat feedback from bosses and colleagues as optional extras or mere fiction. They are not receiving and understanding the plain signals. I call it being on permanent transmission, but with all incoming signals blocked.

## Impression points

Clearly, within your personal brand you make a lot of different impressions. Your personal brand is like a prism with many facets. You see different angles depending on what aspect you look at, but you are always aware of the whole prism. You instinctively know that the prism has a complex structure holding it together, while you can only observe one facet at a time.

Your personal brand is similar: the observer knows you are a complex person with many elements but focuses on only one aspect at any one time. That's the secret of laying down a carefully constructed personal brand. Pay attention to all the facets and make them as good as you can, then the whole structure will be solid, as it is built carefully of high standards in all the aspects of your personal brand. These facets can be seen as **impression points**, and I have identified four major ones:
- First impressions;
- Communication skills;
- Leadership skills;
- Adding value to the company.

## Underlying assumptions

Let's be clear on some assumptions underlying all of this. We are working on your personal brand in your career and you must be aware that work colleagues have serious expectations of you. You have a relationship with them and it's not to be their friend. They work with you, otherwise they would not be here with you, they would be out with their mates. Don't confuse the priority here: colleague first, possibly friend later.

The second assumption is that to develop these impression points you need to look at your behaviours. I suggest that you concentrate on a small number of important behaviours under each impression point, and work to give a very good impression with each.

Finally, being dazzling on one impression point is not enough; to really impress, you must work on all aspects to build a rock-solid personal brand. Beware the case of the strong team leader who impresses the boss with her plans but annoys everyone else, steals their ideas, fakes it, promises much but leaves others to deliver; she will eventually be spotted.

## Impression point: good or bad first impression?

### First impressions do count

Why would you not want to make an excellent first impression? Usually it's because you have not realised how important it is, or is it possible that you are too arrogant to care?

Here are some factors which contribute to the first impression:
- Do you have presence when you meet someone? It is a mix of confidence, high energy, empathy, direct eye contact and body language.
- Do you radiate energy or apathy?

- Do you look the part or skip the part; do you have poise? How well groomed are you? I am constantly telling people it does not matter how casual the dress code is, always default to *great* casual.
- Are you a chameleon or porcupine? Do you dress to adapt, or to make a point? The key thing is to dress one level up, dress to the level to which you want to be promoted.
- Do you radiate likeability or leaveability? People make snap decisions about how likeable you are and it is very hard to come back from these. If you are being dismissive or too hurried to say hello, that will make an indelible impression.
- Do you have empathy or 'me-pathy'? Is it all about you or all about them? Most people think about themselves first, so if you only talk about yourself and don't take any notice of others, they will think you're taking up all the oxygen in the room!
- Ask yourself honestly, are you capable of rudeness? Being too absorbed in the task at hand and not understanding the importance of manners can have unintended bad consequences.
- At events, do you display open or closed behaviours? When you are networking at events, if you gather in a closed clump with your colleagues, forming an impenetrable ring, you will appear completely closed off and part of a clique. Why go to networking events and stay with your pals? These events should be an opportunity to make a good impression on strangers.
- Don't have a limp, corpse-like handshake, but don't crush the other person's hand either; go for firm but appropriate!

All of the above are split-second impressions but have the ability to cause real damage to your personal brand as they can just tick people off.

## Impression point: communication skills

Once you have made the initial impression, you start communicating and in an instant reinforce that impression. Over the years I have found lack of communication skills comes up as the key challenge for executives. The problem can vary, from simple deficiency in techniques like failing to make eye contact to an unintelligible accent. Communication skills are a very potent impression point: they can enhance or damage a whole personal brand in an instant. I have seen someone make a perfectly crafted speech, deliver it with no notes and utterly impress her senior colleagues. I am sure you have seen the opposite, when a brilliant executive stands up and makes such a bad presentation it's like watching a car crash.

Look at these three behaviours – speaking clearly, communicating and talking without props – and how they can influence perception of your communication skills.

## 1. Speak clearly or speak lazily

It might seem trite to start with a plea for speaking clearly, but I'm afraid that elocution teachers are an endangered species. It's not good to use slang in formal meetings and presentations. It's not good to slur your words, mumble or not to know how to pronounce words correctly. I am appalled when intelligent people who may look the part and have the right qualifications, are then unable to speak clearly and throw away an interview, client meeting, etc. This is not often mentioned in feedback, but I have seen it enough to believe it to be an issue nonetheless. You do not have to have BBC pronunciation, but you can't have such an indecipherable accent that no one can understand you. Making a decision to improve on this can instantly improve the impression you are making.

Use of lazy, generalised language gives an impression of being vague. This happens, for example, when you constantly use the word "issue" to describe everything, rather than using more exact words and phrases like "a short-term problem", "an impediment", "a failure of courage", "a clash of personalities", or anything other than an "issue". Retreating into corporate jargon, like: "escalating an issue", "reaching out to people", "sounding it out", "leading out" projects, "sending decks" or "building wireframes", leaves you marooned when you leave your company and need to impress outsiders. Use of jargon within your company could also alienate some staff, or visiting clients who don't use it.

If people have remarked on your way of speaking, you have a clue that you need to act. Make it a priority to increase your vocabulary every day. Read outside your industry, read good fiction, use a dictionary and keep a word book. A word book is an alphabet-indexed notebook in which to write down all the new words you learn. People are impressed by a good use of English; be good at it.

If you really want to excel at written English, get the surprise bestseller *Eats, Shoots and Leaves* by Lynne Truss (Profile Books, 2003) or the *Economist Style Guide*, which is available as a free downloadable PDF.

### Disappointing

Throwing away the chance to shine and showcase your good work with vague or inexact speech.

### Impressive

Carefully chosen language showing you really grasp what you are talking about and that you are trying to communicate in a precise way that helps the listener exactly understand the decision they are being asked to make.

## 2. Communication or talkification? Did they get the message I intended?

The essence of good communication is that the listener gets the exact message you intended to deliver. Look at this example:

| | First speaker | | Listener | |
|---|---|---|---|---|
| **Stage 1** | Meant to say: Your work is good overall, but in this instance I need you to do a new proposal. | Actually said: Your proposal was not good enough, I need a new one. | | |
| **Stage 2** | | | Actually heard: Your proposal is not good enough, I need a new one. | Thought they heard: Yet again, you're not good enough at your work. |
| **Stage 3** | | | Feeling criticised, they become annoyed and react defensively. | |
| **Stage 4** | Take offence at what they perceive as unnecessary defensiveness and accuse listener of being *too* self-protective. | | | |

|  | First speaker | Listener |  |
|---|---|---|---|
| **Stage 5** |  | Register this as a further attack and think the first speaker is behaving aggressively and unreasonably. |  |
| **Stage 6** | Upset, with original message lost. | Upset, with original message lost. |  |

People make sense of communication using more than the exact words used: they look at your body language, your intonation, your pauses and your inflection points. This is very clear when one is with a bully. We all know when we are being bullied, even though experienced bullies are expert at choosing non-offensive language: the threat lies in every other aspect of their communication. They mock or intimidate with voice and gesture.

**Talkification** is when a person says a lot but means very little. You frequently hear company chairpersons defend the indefensible at AGMs. Please don't think that talking means communicating. I regard politicians as the worst users of talkification. Listen to them when they are under pressure from a good interviewer or being forced to apologise. Don't fall into the trap of thinking you can talk yourself out of difficulty. If you don't know the answer or have not done the work, say so. No one wants the brand attribute of being a waffler!

In an instant you can lose credibility by talking at people and failing to really ensure your listener has got your message. The opposite, when someone really speaks to you, engages you, looks at you and stays until you are clear on their meaning, makes a huge positive impression.

If you want clear communication to be a hallmark of your personal brand, the solution is to be careful of all of these aspects. Use 'clean' English, by that I mean only those words needed to convey your message. You get this when you strip out all the hidden meanings, emotional phrases and personal biases. Instead of saying, "If you are not too busy and won't mind, I would like you to write a short report for me, but not like your last long-winded one", instead say "Please prepare a 1,000-word status update, including financial implications, on progress on the project between month one and month four, by 5 pm on Friday." No emotion, no rebukes, no sarcasm and no personal dislike.

Everyone I know who has found communicating difficult has marvelled how the use of clean English improved their communication instantly. It is a simple and immediately useable tool.

It is vital to check with the person that they have received your communication as you intended, ask questions, and clarify frequently. This is especially important if you work in a hierarchical work structure, like medicine or the army, where people obey your communications to the letter.

### Disappointing

Covering up lack of knowledge with lots of waffle and believing that people can't see through it.

### Impressive

Seeing an effective, succinct call to action by a leader, followed by clear questioning until the person is certain there is no ambiguity or unanswered concerns among the audience.

## 3. Can I talk without props?

Are you a jaded PowerPointer? Are all your messages delivered in decks? Are the images you use from Clip Art or Free Photos? Have you forgotten how to write full sentences?

If you really want to stand out, you must be capable of delivering any message without the support of slides. Doing so forces you to really understand your content, build a logical flow and cut out unnecessary padding. It is a sad sight to see a senior executive reduced to silence when his laptop malfunctions and he cannot deliver the message without slides. It looks like he doesn't know what he's doing and this makes a lasting bad impression.

If you must use slides, don't start your preparation by opening PowerPoint and working on the first slide. Draft your message first in a logical sequence and then build a presentation to deliver it. Don't just prepare a lot of slides and hope that makes a presentation. You need the slides to be a backup, not to overwhelm you.

I spend a lot of my time telling people to dump 30 of their 35 slides. Remember this simple point: if you have 30 minutes to present you can make 30 points at one minute each. That's it. Therefore, if you prepare 50 slides, thinking you will flick through them, you will run over time. Is it not the worst feeling when the presenter says, "I only have 20 more slides" as his allotted time ends? Everyone's heart sinks and you'd be prepared to pay him to stop.

I have had this experience when I gave a speech to a conference and the speaker before me was to end his 45-minute speech at 12.15. I was to speak from 12.15 to 1.00, ending at lunch hour. He had about 60 slides, which seemed more like 600, and when it came to 12.15 he kept talking. He kept apologising, but still kept talking, and finally ground to a halt at 12.35. Not only did he take 20 minutes of my time, but he made me the speaker who was keeping the audience from their lunch. His problem was that he allowed the slides to control him: as far as he was concerned he had 60 slides and he was going to deliver them, whatever happened. I reckon if the whole audience had left he would have still kept going. He had a great message but his 'death by PowerPoint' presentation ruined it.

Recall Mark Twain's famous saying "I didn't have time to write a short letter, so I wrote a long one instead". Clarity and succinctness are personal brand definers. There's no better way to be concise than by painting word pictures – using powerful metaphors to engage people and make your message memorable and different.

### Disappointing

Covering up lack of ideas with a boring PowerPoint statement of the obvious.

### Impressive

Clear, engaging communication, entirely without slides, by someone who explains the core of an idea and what they want everyone to do when the talk is over.

## Impression point: leadership skills

I would like to tackle one myth at the beginning of this section on leadership skills. I've discovered that many executives do not really understand the difference between management and leadership, so I would like to tell you what I see as the difference before we go any further. Understanding the difference and changing your behaviour accordingly will be a defining enhancer of the impression you make. That is the first of five behaviour changes I recommend; the other four are to build meaningful relationships, build your stickability, develop sensitive not frustrating behaviours, and always promise less and deliver more.

## I. Be clear on the difference between leadership and management behaviours

Every time I introduce this concept to an audience of executives and ask them to tell me which they are, I am amazed at all the self-declared leaders I find in the room. Yet, in discussions of the reality of their work, these same people admit to the daily behaviours of a manager, rather than a leader. The joint pressures of corporate deadlines and demanding bosses often move people into the reactive, detailed task-manager approach.

Which do you think you use? Let's start with assessing where you spend most of your time. Use the 80–20 rule to guide you: which style do you use 80% of the time? This will give you a good first sight of what type of leadership brand you have. Look at the following table and under each question decide what percentage of your time you spend in A and in B. Mark it on the table.

| YOUR BRAND STYLE OF LEADERSHIP/ MANAGEMENT | A | What % of your time do you spend in A? | B | What % of your time do you spend in B? |
|---|---|---|---|---|
| What do you prioritise? | Change | | Stability | |
| What do you put first? | Leading people | | Managing work | |
| Where is your primary focus? | Long-term | | Short-term | |
| What do you see on your horizon? | Vision of the big picture | | Immediate objectives | |
| How do you lead people in work? | Setting direction and letting people go work on the details | | Planning the details for them | |

| Your Brand Style of Leadership/ Management | A | What % of your time do you spend in A? | B | What % of your time do you spend in B? |
|---|---|---|---|---|
| Do you: | Facilitate decisions by people? | | Make decisions for them? | |
| Is your approach: | Proactive? | | Reactive? | |
| How do you persuade? | Sell | | Tell | |
| How do you cope with risk? | Take risks | | Minimise risk | |
| What do you do with conflict? | Use it | | Avoid it | |
| What do you do with blame? | Take it | | Give it | |

Leadership behaviours are listed in column A, so depending on how many ticks you have in column A, you have just rated what percentage of your time you spend in leadership mode. How does it compare to your first guess? Are you like my audiences, who overestimate the time they spend behaving as leaders?

This insight must be the beginning of you taking charge of this impression point: **you will stand out if you question your established practice and take steps to routinely behave more like a leader**. Managers of work are commonplace; leaders of people with a longer-term, bigger vision are the exception.

What percentage of his time do you think Adam, whose story we saw in Step 1, spent in leadership behaviours? He was clearly leading a new process which was challenging stability, but concentrated on managing the work in the short term with an eye on the immediate objective. He planned and made decisions for people without listening to them. He told them what to do, minimised risk, created upset, but did not handle the conflict. Sadly for him, he got the blame. And he thought he was a leader!

## 2. Build meaningful relationships

One of the most important skills in business is the ability to build meaningful and lasting relationships. This is one of the most valuable skills you can develop. The fundamental behaviours are obvious: to develop a meaningful connection, you need to treat people with respect and be more of a giver than a taker. It's easy to do this within your circle of comfort, with your own team and immediate colleagues; the real challenge is to go outside of that. This is particularly difficult if you are deskbound, as you can sit all day and never interact personally with people on different floors. I have seen people fail to interact with people four rows away in an open-plan office.

There is no point having a wonderful personal brand if no one knows about it and you have failed to reach out and build personal connections.

Doing your work is necessary, but that only gets you so far, as all business, when stripped back to the essentials, is about doing business with other **people**. There are a number of people who will have a profound effect on your career; they are the people you build relationships with today. People change divisions, companies, countries, and as you build relationships with these people your personal brand will spread.

The power of being able to link into genuine connections across the corporate world is a brand definer. The skill is in making them; the behaviour is in reaching out today and tomorrow and making the connection.

Map out the significant people you need to build relationships with in your company. This is the first step; then you need to find ways of interacting with them. I explore this in greater detail in Step 7 on building your matrix.

### Disappointing

Seeing someone completely cut themselves off from everyone and concentrate only on the work.

### Impressive

Seeing the power of relationships working when a former colleague gives genuine support to someone's career and recommends them for a job.

## 3. Build your stickability

Being able to stick to the work is an underrated skill. I call it 'stickability'. You see it when someone finishes off the details and just never leaves loose ends. They stick to the work until it is completely done. They behave like the tortoise in Aesop's fable about the tortoise and the hare.

The opposite of stickability is people for whom nothing sticks: details are irrelevant, and they are racing ahead on to the next big thing. They behave like the hare. In the long run, tortoises make it over the line and hares get lost in the bushes. I have a colleague who tells me that she always puts a tortoise with every hare when she is organising teams. Flashes of brilliance are great, but most business careers are built on delivering results consistently.

I have seen some hares come unstuck over the years. A few years ago, I witnessed someone work really hard to negotiate an agreement with a fractious trade union. There were long nights and multiple negotiations, but it was all ruined by the behaviour of a hare-like boss who rushed to the end and signed off before all the details were tied down. He was bored of it all and wanted to go home. It took the union three weeks to unravel the slapdash deal. By that time the boss was on to a new deal, leaving the tortoise to tidy up, as always. It did not seem to strike him that the new deal would be worthless if costs were not cut with union agreement. The need to move fast was paramount.

In an instant, the behaviours of a hare can make a really bad impression. It is wise to build your skills of stickability through consistent, business-like behaviour.

### Disappointing

Watching a dizzy hare ruin perfectly good work through impatience.

### Impressive

Watching a tortoise who runs a project, containing a dominant hare, managing them by only allowing them small bursts of energy, and so keeping the project on deadline.

## 4. Develop decisive, not frustrating, behaviours

To be a good leader in a company that is contracting, letting people go and cutting all resources, as many are right now, requires you to behave in a sensitive way. Today, there have been whole layers of management taken out by redundancies and with less staff doing more work you now see people thrust into serious situations needing quick decisions. Often, they are untrained and unprepared for the new speed of decision-making. I have seen this across all sectors, but especially in the public sector, where outsourcing is no longer an option. Hard decisions need to be made, decisions that will make you unpopular, require courage and that you may personally dislike. Yet they need to be made and it is your job to make them.

This is where we tend to see inexperienced people use pleasing behaviours and hiding from reality. They don't know how to handle the difficult job of prioritising and delivering with fewer resources. But pleasing behaviour becomes frustrating behaviour if there is a failure to face hard truths and take decisions that will upset people. In this light what was their conciliatory behaviour now looks like indecision.

I always advocate gracious behaviour as a hallmark of an excellent personal brand, but recently I have seen too many examples of this behaviour. People's personal brands are in real difficulty in such situations. If you are intent on being the 'nice' guy, even in a difficult situation, you may reach your limits and this can lead to so much stress that you end up on stress-related leave. It goes beyond personal brand damage to real career damage.

### Disappointing

Seeing a person's brand damaged because they cannot make decisions.

### Impressive

Watching someone show grace under pressure and keep their dignity even in very awkward circumstances.

## 5. Promise less and deliver more

The worst damage to a personal brand is to get a name for not delivering what you promise. I have worked with people on rescuing a personal brand damaged by their failure to deliver to their boss something vital which they promised. (This may be due to many reasons: poor time-management or lack of prioritisation. You can upskill to correct these, but it is more worrying if it is due to lack of motivation.) They owned up to the behaviour, promised to work on it and then proceeded to behave in the same way in our programme. The behaviour was so ingrained that it had become unconscious.

Look around you: haven't you seen this behaviour at some time in your career, and can't you recognise the words used to describe it?

"Unreliable", "needs watching", "needs false deadlines", or "needs close scrutiny".

I have witnessed a remarkable example of this behaviour repeated over a number of years and tolerated because when the person's own interests crossed with a business need and they applied themselves, magic happened, and they delivered stunning results. However, when a new CEO was appointed the business changed, and this person's idiosyncratic behaviour was no longer tolerated and, much to his surprise, he was let go. Make it a hallmark of your personal brand to **promise less and deliver more**.

I have worked with people to improve a bad reputation for not delivering. A major reason for this is that people like the excitement of planning and holding strategising meetings with lots of stakeholders. They can get carried away in the moment and promise many things. Then the excitement passes and the boring detailed work has to be delivered. Unfortunately, the person has become bored and does not want to do the less exciting work. The answer lies in realising that all jobs have this balance of the exciting and the mundane. Sometimes when people realise that they have this reputation it comes as a big surprise to them, as they were genuinely unaware of the impression it was making on their boss. The realisation went a long way to helping them change.

### Disappointing

Watching someone who is unaware that they consistently over-promise, and does not realise the damage this behaviour is doing to their brand.

### Impressive

Seeing someone rescue a damaged brand by owning up to this and working hard to deliver projects on time.

At this point you will have seen that first impressions do count, and that communication and leadership skills are a vital part of how you make a lasting great impression. I believe that a powerful impression point is to be seen as someone who adds value to the company. It really does make you stand out among your colleagues.

## Impression point: adding value to the company

It is an invaluable skill and a powerful personal brand enhancer to be able to add value in your work. There are a number of behaviours that will help you build this skill. It is useful to be a thoughtful contributor who adds to the success of meetings rather than a passenger – people notice if your contributions are intelligent and useful. A clear win lies in being clear about your challenges and not hiding, as people will find out your deficiencies and think the less of you because you were not honest. Value comes when you are a real worker and you focus on results but work in a way that allows others to come along with you.

Here are seven key behaviours that help create a real impression of adding value to your colleagues' work and to the company.
1. Be thoughtful, not silent.
2. Don't hide in plain sight.
3. Do it, don't fake it.
4. Focus.
5. Never make it 'my way or the high way'.
6. Solve the problem, don't add to it.
7. Provide business intelligence, not business-speak.

### 1. Be thoughtful, not silent

I know it's better to remain silent and be thought a fool than to speak and remove all doubt! However, you can take that too far. I remember being told about a situation where a team leader had watched his team file into the back row at a briefing with the newly arrived Vice President. The otherwise impressive team had behaved like school kids and had snuck into the back and hidden. They were afraid to be spotted, they didn't ask any questions, failed to make any impression on the VP and they let him down. Zero for their brand impression, and an own goal for their boss.

I appreciate we have a culture in Ireland of "being backwards about coming forwards", but surely the time for this has passed. If you want to make a name for yourself and stand out, being one of the silent majority is not the way to do it. Some people go to meetings because they have to; just being present is enough for them. I appreciate that you may need to be seen to be present at meetings, but if you have nothing to add, then why are you there? Earlier in my career I worked with boards of many community and development groups across the world and I could never reconcile the amount of money spent on meetings. They achieved little because the board members were there as organisation representatives and saw their role as protecting their organisation's interests above all else. There was no interest in meaningful debate or inquiry. Many of the board members I met never thought of being insightful, thinking strategically or questioning prevailing opinion. The clue was often in how regularly they turned up totally unprepared and without their board papers.

If you are in an organisation that has lots of meetings with loose agendas, you will stand out if you begin to behave differently. Don't call these meetings. Always do thorough preparation and demand insights and valuable contributions from everyone present.

A good way to contribute at meetings is to be the one who summarises and makes suggestions for the next stage. If self-interested parties go into standoff positions, be the one who offers a new alternative and moves it along. You will be noticed.

Sitting silently is not a personal brand-building exercise. At best you are invisible, at worst you lack opinions. At the risk of being sexist here, I have seen this as being a problem affecting more women than men. Many women tell me that they don't want to be seen as butting in: if a dominant group opinion emerges, they feel unable to contradict it. In a male dominant group they often retreat from what they see as male bravado. If you are a woman in this situation you need to read **Step 8** on holding and leaking power.

### Disappointing

Seeing intelligent people sitting back and watching less talented people dominate meetings, then complaining about it later at their desks.

### Impressive

An otherwise quiet executive making a difference when he sums up in a fair and conciliatory way and brings fractious and divisive people from different departments to a novel and face-saving compromise.

## 2. Hiding in plain sight

Have you seen people who work for you hiding in plain sight? By this I mean that they are not being forthcoming with all the information you need. For example, when something simply does not make sense you are usually missing some piece of information. If you, as a team leader, need to account for all your activities and are in a metrics-driven business, you are in grave danger when your support staff are hiding things from you. You can look as if you do not know what is going on. When you see that they can't solve easy problems, you go through stages in your head, first questioning their skill, then their commitment, your instructions and finally their competence. You cannot believe people might be hiding things from you; you believe the best, at first; after all you don't routinely lie by omission, so why would you suspect others do? But you should.

I came across this potential personal brand damage when working with someone whose whole support team had been outsourced overseas. He slowly realised that their work was falling behind; they kept telling him all was well, but the data was telling him otherwise. Yet, in every conversation they promised him that all was improving, they were actively solving the problems, all would be well. He learned a real lesson when he realised that he had never received the whole truth. He thought he saw the whole situation, but he was being outsmarted and fed partial information all the time. The outsourced team did not want to admit they were not delivering. They were afraid they would lose the contract. They choose to fudge and hide the reality and not ask for help. They were hiding in plain sight.

By lying to him, they confused him. He saw that his metrics were off and backlogs were developing; his personal brand was being damaged as he looked like he could not deliver. It looked like his end-of-year review would be poor.

When he reframed his understanding and he saw that his group were concentrating on protecting their own brand to keep the contract and that that was their sole priority, he changed his approach. He went behind all the excuses and followed his gut feeling that they were hiding more than they were telling. He changed the way he engaged with them so that they could no longer hide behind obfuscation. He set firmer targets, reviewed them daily and weekly, and made them work hard to regain his trust.

### Disappointing

The insult to your intelligence that you will not see the reality because of the sand being thrown in your eyes.

### Impressive

Personal brand rehabilitation when you demand, and get, transparency from people whose work is directly affecting your personal brand.

## 3. Do it, don't fake it

Respect other people's intuition. Most people can see through a fake, it's subliminal. You can act as confident as you like, but over time if you are faking it, people will see through you.

Sharp, insightful senior managers (yes, they do exist) do not like fakery. Everyone is allowed a learning curve when they start a new job, but then you need to own up if, after a few months, you are still not sure about some aspects of your responsibilities. If you are caught out lying and covering up, your brand will be more severely damaged than if you admit to your need for specific advice.

Aim for an authentic personal brand where you are trusted to know the limits of your own capability and expected to look for help when you are genuinely in trouble. **Credibility** is a key personal brand attribute.

I have seen a number of sales people, in different companies, who had been promoted during the Celtic Tiger when product or service sales were through the roof and their sales division was booming. They rose as the sales rose. Responsibilities and territories got bigger, but there was no time given to commensurate training and development. When the economy slumped, these people's empires contracted, departments merged and suddenly they were in charge of new functions, new and demoralised staff, and with biting targets. They had survivor's guilt; they were glad to still have a job, even if it was unrecognisable to them. They felt this was not the time to say, "I am lost"; they didn't seek help either internally or outside the company; they just faked it.

Being a survivor with a fake brand is not a good way to build a career.

### Disappointing

Getting away with faking competence under a mask of belligerence towards anyone who challenges them.

### Impressive

Seeking training or advice to upskill when you find yourself out of your depth; most impressive is paying for it yourself when the company can't or won't.

## 4. Focus

Questioning the obvious is a good trait, but endless questioning and wanting to avoid being pinned down at all costs is not. Getting a reputation for not accepting things at face value is useful as you will often be sent in at the beginning of a project to brainstorm problems and possibilities. Open, creative thinkers are rare and often get to work at the exciting opening stages of projects rather than the duller, more tedious detail stage. If you have this gift, then leverage it, and make it a defining feature of your personal brand.

Where it can adversely affect your personal brand is if you can't switch off this approach. No one gets to do the sexy, innovative work all the time; everyone has to do the basics at some stage. Nothing upsets people more than creative thinking **at the wrong time**.

My most recent example of this wonderful attribute causing problems was an accomplished advertising executive who simply could not make up his mind about his career priorities. He seemed to be developing ADHD, so great was his need for more and more alternatives. He began to appear indecisive, rather than inquiring. He realised that he had to choose his priorities; the act of choice for him was the same as closing off possibilities. He actually felt hemmed in.

I find that it can be more of a problem to have a never-ending flow of ideas than to be limited in your imagination. The cacophony of ideas in your head can be paralysing. It is vital to gather all the ideas and impose a priority on them. You cannot do them all at once, so list them in order and proceed like this: start work on the top three, lose the bottom three and park the ones in between for a number of weeks.

### Disappointing

Talent being wasted due to failure to decide on priorities from among your many ideas.

### Impressive

Learning how to shut down the ideas mill in your head and decide on one priority.

## 5. Never make it 'my way or the high way'

Decisiveness and conviction are vital to developing a leadership brand, but when that tips into certainty there is a potential for personal brand damage. The older I get, the less certain I become about most things. If you lay down the law, impose your convictions all the time and struggle to deal with other people's views, you may be in danger of being seen as a bit of a bully.

It is easy to see the 'my way or the high way' trait in others and I frequently hear it as a lament about a difficult boss. What is harder is to spot this tendency in yourself. A good clue is when your pronouncement is met with silence, the absence of argument and bowed, resigned heads.

I find this very prevalent in the older professions, like medicine and law, where people are paid to be certain in their professional opinions. They are trusted and depended on to give definitive diagnoses or legal opinions. Sadly, this can make them truly bad people managers. The shift into working with teams or juniors can be too hard for them.

I marvel at how these god-like figures make such bad role models for those following them, and yet they can be revered. I see them having very poor personal brands, but it is only when people outside their circle of comfort tackle them that they have to address it.

### Disappointing

Seeing career reward for bad leadership behaviour.

### Impressive

The stand-out leader who calls out their peers for bad leadership behaviour.

## 6. Solve the problem, don't add to it

If you are having difficulty in work or are not progressing as you expected, ask yourself whether you may be seen as adding to problems. People may be leaving you out of prime assignments or not telling you things because they see you as being more trouble than help. As things get tighter in companies there are higher expectations and lower levels of tolerance for 'difficult' people.

I can't believe the number of people who place their own emotional needs right in the middle of a situation, just when professional detachment is what is needed. How many times have you seen a deadline loom and when everyone needs to put in extra effort you find someone choosing that moment to make a point about work–life balance and insist on going home?

If you allow emotional responses to work issues to run your career, you will be seen as a problem. I have seen examples of supervisors shouting at people, or cancelling their subordinates' trips because they did not want to be left in charge of something they were unsure of and without their 'people' sitting there ready to answer all questions. They thought it better to get angry, throw a tantrum and insist on a virtual lockdown of staff than risk exposure as not being on top of everything.

The number of full-blown temper tantrums I hear about from my clients is too many not to be a clear trend. You may think it looks like being the boss, demanding respect and driving results, but in reality you are seen as a huge problem.

You don't want people being happier when you are out of the office.

### Disappointing

The damage to people's confidence when worn down by a boss's bad behaviour; they internalise the issue and fail to see the boss as the real problem.

### Impressive

Anyone who calls out bad behaviour and forces the problem person to own the consequences.

## 7. Provide business intelligence, not business-speak

We have a lot of information, a lot of data, and precious little business intelligence today. When I say 'business intelligence', I mean valuable information extracted from carefully analysed raw data. Many of my clients are drowning in information, and go from one meeting to the next in a fog of unprocessed information. Their bosses want and encourage them to add value to the business and a striking way to do that is to begin asking new questions.

You will immediately stand out if you stop and begin looking for ways of seeing something new. Take what you know and ask new questions, look for patterns, aggregate data and find trends. Find ways of offering your data in new ways to other people. An example of this was when a person in an international company began analysing her information on financial transactions, very basic to her, and began offering it to her colleagues in sales functions across other continental divisions in the company. The sales people were unused to seeing information presented in this way. They only saw this data as being something for accounts; they had never seen the data transformed into something useable. She had given them actionable business intelligence, and so they saw her in a new light. Over a few months this person's name began to come up as 'one to watch' in the company.

If you change from informing people with unanalysed information and move to being known for succinct and insightful content, you will stand out. Busy executives value meetings run by people who set the scene with summary data, equip them with clear indicators of trends, and outline implications of each decision requested. This one change will give you a stand-out personal brand.

### Disappointing

Intelligent people not bothering to ask new questions about what is in front of them.

### Impressive

Seeing someone taking an old and seemingly intractable problem and, by providing new analysis, allowing new solutions to be proposed.

## And finally: be gracious

Can you remember the last time you received a card or small gift in thanks from someone in business? Do you remember when a very senior person called you or sought you out and personally thanked you? It's not always about money and bonuses: it's also about recognition – genuine recognition, not company merchandise that sits on our desks and hangs on our walls. Believe me, the occasional, personally chosen and timely gift is remembered long after the hundreds of brilliant reports have been shredded.

I realised I felt very strongly about this from my experiences of cultivating potential philanthropists when I was with the Arthritis Foundation. We did not call it anything so grand then, we just knew we had to catch these rich people's attention and when we did, to really thank them for contributing to the organisation. I went to great lengths to think of very special ways, not linked to money or value, to show our appreciation. I saw how much that extra thought meant to people who are used to attention. The power of thoughtfulness stuck with me.

The opposite is also memorable: when you go out of your way to accommodate someone and they take you for granted. Think of the times you wrote a reference for someone, really coached them for a big presentation, and they never thanked you.

### Disappointing

Receiving fake thanks proffered by someone who is paid to give it on behalf of someone else, or receiving no thanks at all.

### Impressive

A small, genuine show of appreciation from a seriously busy person.

Now that you have taken on board how your behaviour can turn your brand around in a minute, and how to avoid damage by not being mindful enough, I want to be very clear that it is as important to stop behaviour that damages your personal brand as it is to develop impressive behaviours. It is not always about developing new behaviours – sometimes just extinguishing bad behaviours leads to a huge improvement. Think of the difference it makes when someone stops waffling, failing to deliver and starts being concise and delivering on deadline.

This leads me to introduce you to the next step of building your personal brand: the concept of how even a really good behaviour can derail your personal brand if it goes into overdrive.

# Step 5

## Don't let your personal brand drivers derail you

*"People will forget what you said, people will forget what you did, but people will never forget how you made them feel."*

Maya Angelou

- ® **Personal brand drivers**
- ® **The driver**
- ® **The reward for you**
- ® **Excellence**
- ® **Going too far**
- ® **The derailer**
- ® **Recovery**

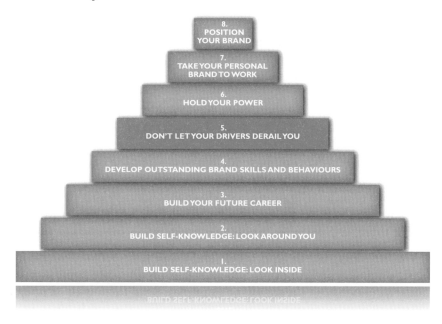

## Personal brand drivers

Some people have strong personal brands with distinctive features. As you observe them at work you are struck by certain attributes and behaviours, like perfectionism, high levels of aggression, people-pleasing or resistance to change. You observe that their personal brand becomes hijacked by a small set of behaviours. This behaviour is the most striking thing you remember about them. You can probably think of someone whose personal brand behaviours can be succinctly described in one word or phrase: 'the nit-picker', 'the one who must be obeyed', 'the energy drainer', 'the moaner', or 'the fun lover'.

I would like to introduce you to a range of personality drivers and show you situations I have observed where the personality driver that gets you noticed and promoted can, if allowed to go out of control, limit or derail a career.

I have worked with executives who have reached a mid-career crisis. They have reached a certain level, senior manager or director, and then plateaued. Examples I have seen include: going for the logical next step promotion and not getting it, looking for a transfer to another division and failing, standing outside the partnership group and not being invited in, or applying repeatedly for high-profile team leads and being refused.

They often tick all the boxes: they are technically proficient, they have the necessary experience and exposure to the business, they have progressed steadily up the career path, but something is clearly stopping them. Their personal brand will not take them to the next level because it is damaged in some way.

## Personal brand drivers and derailers

To make this real for you I have highlighted here nine personal brand drivers and explained how they can become derailers. A 'personal brand driver' is an overriding behaviour that actually drives the person's brand; the person is known for this behaviour and it comes to define them.

If you are struggling in your career and think your personal brand is being damaged or is in crisis, you will gain insights into some of the underlying causes in the following examples. Read them with an open mind and see where you find yourself. The examples are: 'attentive to detail'; 'likes helping people'; 'likes to deliver results'; 'individual and creative'; 'a listener'; 'vigilant and cautious'; 'optimistic and forward-planning'; 'passionate'; or 'a facilitator'.

My approach to explaining each of the nine brand drivers is to give you a telling phrase used frequently in conversation. I will explain what the driver is and the reward for you in cultivating it. I will show how it can be a mark of excellence for you in your career, up to a point, and then pinpoint how, if it goes too far, it can damage and derail you. I will then give you pointers for recovering.

If you think your personal brand is damaged or you see yourself as blocked, reading this step will give you a valuable insight and will allow you to begin to rebuild your career momentum.

## 1. Underlying personal brand driver: attentive to detail

The telling phrase: *"Just do it one more time to eliminate that last bug!"*

You see the entire scope of a project and all the sub-steps. You like to be in control of all aspects. You set the goal of excellence for all steps and you do not compromise easily on standards, if at all. You have such an exacting approach that most people do as you ask rather than incur your displeasure, which is always near the surface.

You often speak of being irritated, particularly by other people's failure to see that your way is the correct way. Your reputation for being hard to please and having high standards spreads and defines your personal brand.

### Reward for you

Employees, suppliers, contractors learn that you have high standards, do not tolerate mistakes and will keep sending work back until it is up to your standard. You therefore get the best work sent to you, because people are wary of disappointing you.

### Personal brand excellence

If you keep this up, you will get a reputation as a hard taskmaster and your brand will be associated with high standards. You are often called in when reviews are being done and when nit-picking is considered a necessity. You find every problem, every slip in standards; you make the best quality control person. When the pursuit of the 1% improvement is needed, you are the master!

### Going too far: derailing

In pursuing total excellence you find yourself focusing on the last 1%. When you fail to notice the 99% and only see the 1%, you are beginning to derail.

If you focus on the perfect result but fail to take other things into account, like deadlines, limited resources, sense of urgency or the people you have exhausted, you are derailing into the hell of absolute perfectionism for its own sake. It's no longer serving the business interest and is now solely about you. This highlights you as inflexible, not business savvy, overly demanding, poor at understanding and motivating staff, and difficult!

You can become known as a demotivating boss from hell, who never praises and is never satisfied.

### Recovery

- Beginning to put things into the correct proportion is the first step.
- Learn how to prioritise the issues you demand perfection on and to ease back on the others. Everything can't be a priority.
- Try to encourage and incentivise rather than demand better results.
- Investigate causes of low standards and put in long-term fixes rather than thinking that being demanding will encourage improvement. This builds on the point in the previous step of the value of genuine thanks and appreciation – starting to offer this is good for your brand.

## 2. Underlying personal brand driver: likes helping people

The telling phrase: *"If you don't mind/I would appreciate/If it's not too much trouble."*

You like people and you need them to like and approve of you. You always focus first on the people in a project, then on technicalities and the results needed. You are intuitive in your evaluation of a person's state of mind and well-being, so you can easily read people and their moods.

### Reward for you

You get on well with people. You find this easy. Your subordinates like you, you seem to understand them. You charm them, rather than boss them, so they like pleasing you and all is well when there is an even flow of work and no real pressures. This approval feeds your self-confidence. The more others approve of you, the more worthy of approval you believe you are.

### Personal brand excellence

You get a reputation for building happy environments, cooperating teams and lasting relationships with other departments. In short, staff and clients love you.

### Going too far: derailing

When seeking approval takes over as the prime driving force above all else, you begin to derail. You get a reputation as a pleaser and that you are soft on people. This escalates in pressurised work environments and when deadlines are tight.

Those around you fail to perform, knowing you will never tackle them on it; they learn how to control you. They like you, but that does not mean they will put your requirements ahead of theirs. You have created a cycle of behaviours: you apply pressure, your staff or suppliers ignore it and carry on as normal, more pressure is applied to you as things are not moving fast enough, you pass the pressure down but they continue to soft-soap you and play on your conflict avoidance. This continues until you either snap or give up. If this continues through a few cycles, you can see how you will have damaged your reputation. You can now be seen as a non-deliverer of work.

Too much people-pleasing backfires in a crisis when you have to put the work first. It makes enforcing deadlines more difficult and it can create a climate of frustration and hidden resentments. People don't know where they are with you.

You get the reputation of being a pushover; you are too nice, and you have no authority. At worst you become known as a 'Pollyanna'. Consider Gerald's story:

#### GERALD: LOVE ME 'COS I'M NICE

You would think gentleness and charming behaviour would be hall-marks of a great brand, but this story will show you how that can go very wrong.

Gerald was highly intelligent, in his late 30s, well qualified, had a career path through blue-chip companies and had landed in a large multinational. When I met him he was well paid and in charge of a large and diverse group of people. He had arrived, career-wise.

The reality was that he was miserable and failing badly after six months. His personal brand in this new company was suffering damage. Although he had progressed consistently through his career to this point, he had never really learned how to manage people. Up to now this had not been a problem, as he had had a collegiate relationship with a smaller team and was in a loosely managed environment and his people-pleasing charm had gotten him through.

Now Gerald was operating in a different environment, under the eye of a determined and ruthless manager and a greater part of his success came from the results of his large team's work. A crucial aspect was the presence of outside contractors in this team, who needed detailed task and deadline management.

This was a team in name only and was largely a number of independent sub-groups. To succeed, Gerald needed them to deliver on time and to combine their results. This necessity to motivate and lead others was new to him. He realised that he had zero people management skills just when his continued success depended on having them.

Gerald had reached the point where his best brand attribute had just derailed him. His niceness, combined with his conflict avoidance, allowed his people to largely ignore him, as they knew he would never bite.

His boss wanted results and wanted them yesterday. Deadlines came, and despite being shouted at he was not capable of passing the sense of urgency down the line. It was lodging with him. He told me that he could not command credibility and respect from his team. They were ignoring him and he was letting them. The more he tried to please, the more he lost respect.

Gerald felt compressed between the pressure from above and the elusiveness of his team below. He had become the meat in the sandwich. His boss wanted him to grow teeth, like hers. But Gerald wanted to be respected, not feared like his boss. The result was that his personal brand was no longer that of the genial, nice bloke but was alternating between that of a weak kitten and a doormat.

Gerald was allowing his fear of actually managing people – their deadlines, their productivity and lack of engagement – to damage his career. Can you see how his attributes and behaviours had morphed from useful assets to liabilities? His lack of ability to manage up and down had derailed his personal brand.

Our work together centred on rebuilding his personal brand. Gerald needed to return to his signature strengths of empathy, charm, relationship-building, but also learn to manage people and give hard messages. He thought that telling people what to do was bullying. He learnt how to follow up every instruction, make people accountable and still honour his desire to be a nice guy.

He realised that hiding from his boss, always acquiescing to her view, never questioning even when he was correct, had to stop. He turned the situation around.

Gerald's boss subsequently left the company and a true indicator to me that a core brand attribute always rules one's behaviour was that after six months he was in trouble with his new boss. Again, Gerald's people-pleasing was the problem. However, this time it was corrected faster, as he recognised his behaviours quickly and realised he was the problem, not his new boss. He now knew how to solve it.

### Recovery

- Realise that you can be the boss and still be nice; they are not mutually exclusive.
- Work on building your own confidence so you do not need to use the approval of others as a crutch.
- Learn to be constantly assertive and not oscillate between pleasing and aggression.
- Use clean, neutral English and remove all emotion and cajoling language.
- Learn to follow up every request, and make it clear you will always do this.

### 3. Underlying personal brand driver: likes to deliver results

The telling phrase: "*Of course it will be delivered early and under budget, leave it to me.*"

You are an achiever; you seek approval because of your excellent work. You do not do failure; all your projects are on time and to the highest standard. You are a master at designing the fastest route from (a) to (b) and marshalling the resources needed. You have an innate charm and can coax people into cooperating with you so you get what you need.

### Reward for you

You are praised as a doer, a go-getter, a finisher. You get bigger and harder projects because you always deliver and your reputation for delivering results is solid.

### Personal brand excellence

You shine in a results-driven environment. Your rack up the hours, are never sick, never take leave, your job is your life. You pride yourself on never asking anyone to do anything you would not do yourself. Your reputation for results gets you promoted when results matter, especially if a large part of the success depends on your own workaholic schedule.

### Going too far: derailing

You begin to derail when your drive for results takes over and starts to demotivate those working with you. You forget to notice them as human beings; you start to appear like an unforgiving task master. They rightly feel that you are more focused on the outcome than on the people involved.

There is a danger that morale will plummet, absenteeism will increase. You know you are in trouble when staff start leaving in numbers or filing complaints against you. Staff churn rates are often the sign of a workaholic on the loose. Your brand is damaged when you are seen as a work horse, capable of delivering results, but better left out of the promotion track. It's too risky to promote you as you cannot be given responsibility for more people. People start describing you as leaving 'dead bodies' in your wake or 'throwing people under the bus' in pursuit of a result.

### Recovery

- Change from believing your worth comes from what you produce. Instead, believe your worth comes from who and what you are.
- Start noticing how much attention you give to outcomes and how much attention to the people in your work environment.
- Be kinder to yourself, there is more to life than work.
- Realise that you need people around you to deliver: your job is not to singlehandedly save the company, unless you are the only employee!
- Start to trust people around you a little more.
- Remember your way is not the only way, it might be quicker but it pays to listen to others.
- Lastly, a bit of kindness always helps.

### 4. Underlying personal brand driver: individual and creative

The telling phrase: "*I really want to be special and to make a unique contribution.*"

You are a committed, creative person who wants to stand out and be recognised for making a unique contribution. You always look for the unusual angle and offer quirky options. You can think outside the box, but usually on your own terms.

### Reward for you

You form intense relationships with people, look for authentic meaning in these and so you make a great impact. You are valued for your creativity and originality. You search for authenticity and can be seen as being quite an intense person.

### Personal brand excellence

You closely identify yourself with the impression you are making and are very alert to any issues. This can make you very responsive. Your desire for uniqueness will mark you out as a creative thinker and someone willing to try different approaches.

### Going too far: derailing

Because you are very sensitive and creative, you are prone to taking comments to heart. You can fail to maintain detachment and to see the difference between professional and personal comments and may take too much personally. This can trigger emotional responses, leading to you being seen as unprofessional, though you may not realise that your responses are seen as those of a touchy person. The quest for difference may derail you in pushing you to being too precious and not being able to take input from others. The danger is that you may take criticism of your work as being criticism of you as a person. You need to see the difference; your personal brand is in real danger when you blur the two.

If you perceive comments as an attack on you as a person, you put yourself under intolerable pressure and you may lash out at people. Unfortunately, such episodes are remembered.

If you get a reputation for being precious or prickly, you will find other people walking on eggshells around you and couching everything in ways designed not to offend you. You are no longer seen as a contributor but as someone whose moodiness has to be managed. You get the moniker of being 'difficult to deal with'. You may be left out of discussions, meetings, or events as organisers want to remove your contrariness from the process. This in turn may feed your insecurity and so, as things get more strained, you are in a cycle of brand damage: you feel left out and react; they see the reaction and leave you out more.

## Recovery

- It's okay to be unique and creative, but in a business setting, business comes first.
- It's your responsibility to be professional and to leave sensitivity at the door.
- When you feel someone has said something personal about you, try reframing it to check if it's possible that it was not meant personally, it could be that you are *making* it personal.
- Practice professional detachment; remove overly emotional words from your business vocabulary, so change: "I feel" to "I consider"; "I think"/"I am disappointed" to "I am concerned"; "I am upset by" to "I am struck by".

Note some of your most used words here, and then substitute less emotive ones.

## 5. Underlying personal brand driver: listener

The telling phrase: "*I am listening to you in a detached way and deciding if I have enough resources to do that for you.*"

You live with a scarcity viewpoint; you don't believe that there is enough of you to go around. You are always trying to find ways to minimise the demands the world makes on you, on your time, energy and resources. You are always conscious of the limits rather than the expanses of a project. You stay detached and observe, and so learn a lot and get a full perspective. You are often called on for a wise, rational opinion.

### Reward for you

You can offer a detached, objective viewpoint and so you make an impact when rational – not emotional – input is required. You gain a reputation as professional and thoughtful; in a team you will be valued, as you can put the brakes on more impulsive people. You excel at detailed, linear, exacting tasks and are known as a deliverer of same.

### Personal brand excellence

You will gain a reputation for excellence where detached, objective analysis matters. You will be able to see all sides of a proposal and judge it professionally. You will develop a reputation for being a thorough person, often sought out for your wisdom.

## Going too far: derailing

Some work situations are messy and emotional because of the people involved. Tempers flare, egos clash and sometimes you need to engage to resolve the situation. When you remain detached and uninvolved, it looks like you are not doing your job. Your previously detached wisdom can look like you are hiding from the real issues, or worse, not seeing them.

You get derailed when people start going around you or over you to get input because you no longer seem to be on top. Your objectivity becomes a liability as it appears you cannot grasp the reality of the situation. It seems that you are not grasping the personnel issues.

Your brand gets damaged when you appear so detached that you are deemed irrelevant because you lack urgency, commitment and cannot motivate people in a crisis. You can appear as a problem-focused person if you cannot see beyond your own feeling of being overwhelmed. Your need to cope becomes your prime concern and this influences whether you will get involved in a project or not.

You lose the reputation of being a wise observer and gain the one of being an out-of-touch person, who cannot handle the messy people issues.

## Recovery

- You need to engage more actively in talent issues in the workplace.
- Become more aware of the people around you, notice them and interest yourself in their issues.
- Build on your empathy and relationship skills so you can connect with people.
- Get out of your head and into your body.

## 6. Underlying personal brand driver: vigilant and cautious

The telling phrase: *"I will have a look at all the risks and all the problems and see if we can do that for you."*

You are very conscientious and work hard at keeping the organisation safe from risk; you have a talent for spotting problems and threats to the organisation. When you take a look at a project, you're amazed at how easily you can spot all the things that could go wrong. You have difficulty understanding how others can't see the obvious risks.

### Reward for you

You get a reputation for being a good investigator, risk manager and trouble-spotter. So when the company is planning something big and needs an analysis of what's involved – the many steps, the likely issues, the risks, the worst-case scenarios – you are the first person they look for, and you excel. You are often called in to the planning and implementation stages as you will produce a comprehensive plan with every risk logged.

### Personal brand excellence

You get a reputation for digging deep, looking at all sides, going to the worst-case scenario and planning back from there. If a thorough job is needed with an emphasis on risk assessment, you are the one for it. You will keep the team safe.

### Going too far: derailing

In a fast-changing business world some risk is inherent in everything; overemphasis on avoiding it can derail you. You can become the problem person. Risk takers, high achievers, fast-paced colleagues will avoid you, as they see you as the brakes. You can be so focused on all the problems that you can become paralysed and lose the ability to solve one at a time and to let some go.

You can look as if you are not doing your job, not completing things. Your failure to complete is seen simply as that – not as you being vigilant and checking for every possible problem.

Your brand becomes damaged when people interpret your viewpoint as resistance to change. People see you as a blocker and they overlook you; they avoid asking your opinion as they feel you only have one perspective. You get pigeonholed as a 'problem' person. You are never invited to creative, brainstorming sessions, only to the implementation ones. You lose out on the new, exciting projects.

Your brand becomes damaged when you are seen as a one-dimensional, problem-focused person. If you get the reputation of being a negative person, a problem person, or an obstructionist, you are in brand trouble and you start to be left out of the loop. People won't risk having your 'dead hand' on their project.

### Recovery

- It's perfectly acceptable to see problems in a project, but you must be pragmatic. In a fast-paced business world you do not have the luxury of solving them all to your complete satisfaction.

- You must learn to prioritise problems and not try to tackle them all with the same intensity, as that way lies paralysis.
- When you are in meetings you must practice seeing yourself as others see you; see the listener's viewpoint. They can only tolerate listening to problems for so long and then they tune you out.
- Make it a practice to always present a range of solutions with each problem. This has two benefits: it shifts you to solving rather than just listing problems, and it changes your colleagues' view of you.

## 7. Underlying personal brand driver: optimistic and forward-planning

The telling phrase: *"Problem? What problem? It will be all right on the day, I promise you."*

You have an optimistic view of life and don't like to be put under pressure and asked to do routine tasks. You don't like boredom and will do anything to avoid it. You frequently get 'bothered' by people making demands on you. You like fun and novelty and new things. Repetition is hell for you.

### Reward for you

You star at the brainstorming and development phase of a project. You are high energy, infectiously optimistic if you like the project. You are a natural planner and love the challenge of a complex project. You have a natural charm and people warm to you. You are often invited in at the early stages and have a reputation for innovative and challenging input, and success. As a consequence you get chosen to contribute to winning initiatives.

You like to have lots of options, lots of choices, which make you a great dreamer, useful at the envisioning stages of a project.

### Personal brand excellence

Your optimism and broad thinking are noticed. Your optimism gets you noticed by the high achievers; your big thinking endears you to the leaders of the group. You are given scope to take an idea and run with it. Your ability to conceive new ideas is valued: having lots of ideas means we eventually get the best one.

### Going too far: derailing

Your derailing point comes when you keep operating at the exciting big picture level. Inevitably the project goes from the fun, planning stage to the more routine implementation stages. This is your least favoured place. You don't like the routine, you begin to miss your deadlines and miss the detail. You can gloss over the detail for a while, but eventually the nit-pickers combine with the results people and they start chasing you.

Your natural charm and optimism begin to wear thin as you continue to avoid the boring detail and skip to the next shiny project. You cannot follow through and deliver; you keep coming up with new options. You paralyse yourself with choice. You are derailed by your imagination and your ability to keep finding options.

Damage comes when the perfect storm of your visibility on key initiatives joins your tendency to miss deadlines, your failure to close off tasks and your default tendency to hide from people who are demanding results. You can get a reputation for not being a finisher and your reliability is in doubt.

People think you can't make a decision. They tire of your options and want a conclusion, a result. You get a reputation for being a last-minute person – the one who disappears under pressure and never completes a project.

If you combine indecision with lack of attention to boring detail and a tendency to disappear under pressure, you appear as a problem employee, no longer an asset.

### Recovery

- If you start something, finish it, no exceptions.
- Take responsibility for everything you are involved in; I see responsibility as meaning you own it until it is done or passed to the next stage.
- Handle any attention deficit issues by setting personal goals and sticking to them.
- When pressure mounts, do not hide. Do the opposite, contact whoever is chasing you. The paradox is that, once contacted, they don't feel the need to chase you anymore.

### 8. Underlying personal brand driver: passionate

The telling phrase: *"This is the right thing to do. Anything else is unjust."*

You are very passionate about your work. You hold strong views and feel it necessary to express them unreservedly. You have an inner compass guiding you in your decisions and don't feel the need to check in with the views of others. You know the right thing to do, it seems very obvious to you. You thrive on vigorous debate!

### Reward for you

You are a high-energy person with a reputation for getting things done. You are driven and have passion – valuable commodities in a business. You get a reputation for making the impossible happen. You are good at challenging the status quo and will push through change. This is rewarded when the company needs to push forward, grow its business, start in a new country or take emergency measures to face market challenges.

### Personal brand excellence

You become known as the heavy hitter because you make things happen. The company will use your passion where passion is needed; you will be put in charge of work needing this energy and drive. They don't care if you upset people if the longer term gain is more important.

### Going too far: derailing

If you fail to notice the effect you have on others, you will fail to modify your behaviour in different circumstances with different colleagues. You have a greater comfort with anger and aggression than most other people. When you are not getting your way, you can become aggressive; if thwarted, you can become very stubborn and sulky. When you focus on what you believe is right and fail to notice others, you lack empathy. This affects you the higher up a company hierarchy you go, as high positions are all about bringing people with you.

You can appear intransigent, difficult and antagonistic. Your single-mindedness is now a derailer as you get into huge difficulty with people who disagree with you. Your focus on being right begins to backfire as you lose allies and supporters. You lay yourself open to accusations of bullying. People will refuse to work with you. Your reputation becomes all about your behaviour and less about your work.

You cease to be seen as a problem-solver as you appear to have no flexibility. You quickly become the problem. As you become more senior in a company and encounter a lot of executive egos, you will bruise them and end up sidelined by the more versatile and agile performers. You will have high rates of staff turnover as people start to transfer away from you.

I have come across some unacceptable behaviour over the years where I have seen some pretty passionate and committed managers really become derailed. One example was when I heard of a senior executive making a pregnant woman cry and go home from work; this is not a great brand enhancer! Yet this is what can really happen when an over-bearing, aggressive team leader fails to contain their aggression.

Discounting other people's views can really spin out of control in virtual teams where most communication is by e-mail. There is little context, no body language, no smile, just words on a screen. There is potential for huge brand damage here.

When you stand back and print out a string of e-mails that have been sent back and forth, the reason for the deteriorating relationship becomes obvious. The tendency to domineer and insist on compliance is obvious. The softening effect of actual conversation is missing. I have seen people damage their personal brand by being an e-mail bully.

### Recovery

- Constantly check on your effect on others: notice how they look after you finish speaking, watch their body language. You may have won the argument by browbeating them, but you have lost the personal brand war.
- Realise that your view is only one view, not *the* view. Ask for other people's opinions, and really take them into account.
- Lighten up – realise you are not the saviour of the world.
- Pause before you speak, think, slow down your reaction times.

### 9. Underlying personal brand driver: open to all opinions, facilitator

The telling phrase: *"I find it hard to decide as you are all making a very good case."*

You have a unique ability to see everyone's point of view. You have a serenity and peace about you which allows you to observe and listen to others without projecting yourself onto them. This encourages people to be themselves with you. This makes you very good at facilitating and negotiating.

You are very good at seeing other people's point of view. You like to maintain harmony and routine and to keep things as predictable as possible. You like your reputation for being dependable and even-tempered. You like to empathise and support others, and you enjoy being known as a facilitator.

### Reward for you

The reward for you is being seen as a peacemaker and being good at bringing harmony. You are well liked and people open up to you and ask you for advice. You excel at bringing people from differing perspectives together and you enjoy that role. You generally avoid conflict and strive to live in a harmonious world.

### Personal brand excellence

You will be sought out when an easy-going, friendly approach is needed. You will shine when what is needed is compromise, allowing lots of leeway and personal agendas to be met. When the work is all about process and people, and less about demanding results, you will be the one for the job.

### Going too far: derailing

If you go too far into compromise mode and begin to value harmony over all else, you will begin to derail. If you put everyone else's agenda first, you may miss your real priorities. You may appear indecisive and unable to make your own decisions.

This becomes an issue when you need to stand up and lead. Your team may need you to fight for them at senior level meetings and they will not appreciate your ducking any necessary conflict. In a fast-paced environment like a hospital or retail company, personalities have to adapt and change at lightning speed. Egos are bruised and there is little time for harmony. If you withdraw from the conflict, you will be side-lined.

### Brand damage

You can appear lazy, stubborn, withdrawn, switched off and not really committed. You can lose energy and look like you are resisting all instructions. An air of inertia will begin to surround you.

As you withdraw from conflict and fail to impose your will on others you look weaker and weaker. Results-orientated people will avoid you as you will not deliver for them, and high-energy people will be put off by your inactivity.

### Recovery

- You must escape from your inertia.
- Make it a practice to decide to do one thing at a time, and make yourself finish it.

- Make small goals and be tough on yourself to deliver them.
- Do what you decide is best and stop taking everyone else's views into account.

## PERSONAL BRAND NAMES YOU DON'T WANT

Have a look at these deadly personal brand names and do a reality check to see if you are showing any traces of these. Look hard, as there are none as blind as those who do not see.

### The Drama Queen (or King)

The tagline of the drama queen is: *"Wait until I tell you about my drama."*

If you enter every room, start every phone call with an account of what's happening in your world, with special emphasis on all the bad things, you are a drama queen. You are slowly and steadily damaging your personal brand as soon people work out that you revel in drama. They see you "awfulising" every situation and living off the drama. Your personal brand is predictable and ring-fenced by the need to be a victim.

### The Narcissist

The tagline of the narcissist is: *"Hey, look at me."*

We all know the legend of Narcissus and his reflection. If every sentence contains the pronoun "I", look no further. If you bring everything around to you, wake up. People see a personal brand of a love affair between you and you. There is little room for them. You will be excluded, let off groups and you will have the reputation of taking all the oxygen out of the room. Your personality overwhelms all your brains and experience.

### The Overwhelmed Monkey

The tagline of the overwhelmed monkey is: *"Don't come near me, I'm not coping"*.

Are you constantly telling everyone you are overwhelmed by work, pressure, the job? Do you think this makes you look important, vital to operations? Do you believe the place will close down without you? On the contrary, it makes you look like you are overwhelmed by a pack of barking monkeys. You may think you look busy, but others think your personal brand is out-of-control, inefficient and unable to prioritise. In a results-driven company you will look like a loser.

### The Psychic Vampire

The tagline of the psychic vampire is: *"I can't find anything good to say about anyone."*

"Beware psychic vampires" was the most quoted 'Shoeism' from my book, *Shoeisms: Working Woman's Guide to Take Control and be the Sassy, Successful Woman You Know You Can Be* (Morgan James Publishing, 2009). Readers loved the concept of some people being so toxic that they resembled vampires of the mind, sucking all the essence out of you. We can all tell tales of the toxic people we have met along our careers (another book, perhaps), but imagine if people were applying that personal brand label to you. Pause and see where your attention goes: to the good in people or to the bad? Do you go too far and make toxic comments to people?

### The Emperor has no Clothes

The tagline of the emperor has no clothes is: *"I am the boss so do as I say, despite the fact that you think I am wrong."*

When people are afraid to openly question you, or query your priorities, they often go along with you, even though they really doubt your capability. They know you have no clothes but they are afraid to say so. I see this all the time: temperamental, moody people who are out of their depth using aggression and certainty as a cover. They create a climate of 'go along to get along'.

### The Phoney

The tagline of the phoney is: *"Of course, I can do that for you."*

Inside, the phoney has no notion of actually delivering; what you hear is not what you get. This false promise personal brand works for a while but the more astute see through it quickly. You get the reputation of one who can't be trusted to deliver the work on time. You may find yourself left off crucial projects as the powerful cannot trust you to deliver for them and their personal brand. They see your personal brand as damaging to theirs.

You can protect and enhance your personal brand by being aware of how and when an underlying personality driver can shape and/or derail your personal brand.

If you think your personal brand is damaged in any way, if you are getting negative feedback in work and see opportunities for promotion pass you by, you need to seriously look for any derailing behaviour.

When you have done this and you are happy that your behaviours are aligned to deliver your BAA, your progress should be smooth in your career. However, if despite all this work you still consider that you are not progressing as fast as you should be, if you know you are unexpectedly still stalled in your career, you may need to consider the concept of 'holding and leaking power'.

The next step goes into this in some detail, as I have not seen this being discussed in corporate circles as much as it should be. I have found great success with people who suddenly realise that most of their issues arise from leaking too much power. Read on and find out if you are leaking power.

# Step 6

## Hold your power

*"Experience is the name everyone gives to their mistakes."*

Oscar Wilde

- ® **Leaking and holding power**
- ® **Stop leaking power**
- ® **Hold your power strategy**

## Leaking and holding power

Every day in your career you are interacting with other people and you constantly affect each other's moods, behaviours and well-being. I want you to examine how you feel after these interactions. Do you come away from some people feeling exhausted? Do you feel depressed after certain conversations? Do your good ideas evaporate after sharing them with certain colleagues? Did you join a company thinking it was an exciting place and slowly realise that they have sold you a lemon?

I explain this as losing your power. Some people seem to reach in and take the energy right out of you.

This came to my attention when I observed business people who were extraordinary in their own right, holding responsible positions, leading teams, progressing in their career, suddenly becoming lost and non-functional in certain circumstances.

I wondered what had happened to bring this about, and concluded that we all have a level of power inside us but that we can allow others to take it from us. I am talking about perfectly well-adjusted and healthy workers who stop performing to their full potential right in front of your eyes.

## Leaking power

If you notice or become aware of any of the following, you are likely to be leaking power:
- You are not getting appropriate results from your actions.
- You feel powerless to effect change, despite your best efforts.
- You no longer feel in control of your career.
- Someone else is making you distort your behaviour and that's damaging your career.
- People do not ask for your input.
- Colleagues are ignoring you or disrespecting you.
- You are no longer influencing people at meetings.
- Having progressed steadily until now, you are being passed over for promotion.
- Your working environment is progressively decreasing your confidence.
- Despite working hard to build your career, you feel that it's losing momentum.

## Holding power

The beginning of learning to hold power is when you can read the situation around you, analyse what is occurring and know how to stop letting it affect you.

When you are holding your power you feel calm, controlled and in charge of your thoughts and actions, despite what others are doing. You may see others trying to control your behaviours, trying to coerce you, trying to weaken your position, but you do not let them.

## Stop leaking power

I believe that leaking power is a very real threat to maintaining a powerful personal brand. When I first started talking about this to audiences and outlined when and why it happened, and its profound effect on a personal brand, the silence was palpable. I knew I had hit a nerve. Many had experienced it.

Leaking power occurs in three main circumstances:
1. When you have a certain mindset.
2. When your behaviours give away your power.
3. When you work in a wicked environment.

There are some work environments that simply defeat people unless they are aware of what is going on and know how to handle them. Reading this step will show you if you are leaking power, so that you will find when and where you are doing it and stop. I want to show you how you leak power in these circumstances, but more importantly how you can learn to hold onto your power.

### 1. Leaking power through your mindset

I have always believed that one's mindset is one of the most powerful shapers of personal brand. How you view the world greatly affects how you behave and appear to your colleagues in work. I have discovered four particular mindsets that are brand damagers:
- Leaking power to your nemesis.
- 'Joan of Arc' syndrome.
- Pointlessly competing with everyone else.
- Setting up your own career limiters.

#### Leaking power to your nemesis

When you are unhappy in work due to the actions of another person, you can give all of your power to that person. They seem to invade your mind and you find yourself talking about them all the time. Here are some examples to illustrate my point.

##### ANDREW AND MARTHA: LEAKING POWER

Andrew was a manager in a large organisation and we did a programme of personal development for one year. His request to me was simple. He wanted to rebuild his confidence, which he thought had slowly ebbed over the previous three years in this position. As he told his story, one person, Frank, who reported directly to Andrew, figured prominently in every episode. He spent about three quarters of our first session talking about the influence of Frank: how he stole Andrew's energy, hung out of him, turned small tasks into impossible ones, and never took responsibility for his actual duties. As we moved through our time together, he still spoke of Frank, but less and less. Yet this *nemesis* was always in the background. Andrew allowed this person ready access to him at all times. He allowed Frank to sit in on meetings, even though he never contributed. He saw Frank as a weight around his neck, always there, draining his energy through inertia. When Andrew was challenged to distance himself, he said it was not possible. When urged to tackle Frank on not doing his job, he explained that he was doing his best to try. Yet he still complained. It was as if Frank had sucked all his power and stood aloof, holding it. He was a vampire sucking all of Andrew's attention, and yet Andrew could not see or get away from this grip.

Another client, Martha, was introducing a change programme to a group of people who had managed to elude all changes for about eight years and who had become quite embattled in their office off the main site. Martha was intimidated by them, but specifically by the oldest woman in the group. Every time we discussed tactics, she referenced this woman; every time she decided to do something new, she wondered how that woman would react. Martha even started using other members of staff indirectly as 'moles' to get information about this colleague. Her fear of introducing the change programme all crystallised in this one person. She had developed her own nemesis.

I once ran a leadership programme for women in executive roles in a multinational. It was a long established company with an equally long-running male dominated culture. Many of the women I worked with were razor sharp, gifted in many ways and quite powerful in their roles, yet they kept citing two or three difficult older men as huge constraints on their careers. They could have bought and sold these men but they gave their power to them constantly. They cited their behaviours as dominating, their comments as denigrating and their group-think as a barrier. The women second-guessed themselves all the time, running all their ideas through an imaginary meeting of these men and rehearsing what they would say. It was an utterly draining way to proceed. They had created a group nemesis.

## TAKE POWER BACK FROM YOUR NEMESIS

| Description of your nemesis | Exact opposite description | Steps to take back control |
|---|---|---|
| He won't do his job. | I have not clearly agreed a definition of his duties. | Behave in a more detached way and make responsibilities clearer. |
| He follows me around. | I allow him too much access to my personal space. | I may need help to improve as a manager of people. |
| She will not do as I ask. | I have not managed her effectively enough. | You need to stop using her as a reason not to do things. |
| She will wreck any new idea I propose. | Perhaps she thinks I am not making it clear enough so that she can implement it. | Go around her and take charge of the interactions. |
| They don't like me. | They are impervious to you. | You need to stop letting other people have so much control over your career. |
| They disapprove of me. | They are too busy to even notice you. | Get on with your job and ignore them. |

### Nemesis mindset patterns

At the heart of such stories are distinct patterns of thinking:
- taking things too personally;
- looking to others for approval and validation;
- being too porous to other people's comments;
- communicating indirectly, which in turn allows people to slip away from the point;
- fear of any form of conflict, leading to passivity in face of unacceptable behaviour;
- failure to own your part in the problem;
- feeling you have no power to change this situation.

In each case, I asked people to do an exercise in reframing their mindset. I've set out examples above.

Having looked at these examples, now do it for your situation. Use any number of opposite descriptions that you need.

| Your original description of your nemesis | Write an exact opposite description of the situation | Steps to take back control |
|---|---|---|
| | | |
| | | |
| | | |
| | | |

This exercise will loosen the hold the other has on your thinking, as you begin to see that you just need to take charge. Do not displace your problems onto another person. Once you see your role at the centre and began to take back power, you'll reduce the power of your nemesis.

The key learning is to recognise when you are obsessing over another person's effect on your life; examine your interactions and change your behaviour. It may help you if you consider the whole role of trust here. If you trust others with small things first, you can gradually build them up to taking responsibility, which makes you comfortable, as you have seen evidence of their capabilities on a small 'safe' project already.

### 'Joan of Arc' syndrome

A second mindset I have noticed among ambitious executives which can seriously damage their personal brand is the 'Joan of Arc' syndrome. They like to take full responsibility for everything and everyone. It makes them feel indispensable, but poses real dangers. Taking full responsibility means you:

- Miss the big picture and get embroiled in everyone's details.
- Work below your pay grade and bring everyone down a level.
- Demotivate others by giving them permission to duck responsibility and leave things to you.
- Cover up other people's mistakes.
- Compensate for other people's deficiencies.
- Teach everyone not to finish things.
- Stifle creativity.

You lose all your power as the leader because everyone sees you as the fixer of small things. Any power of real leadership and strategic thinking that was attached to your personal brand as a leader evaporates. I have seen careers wrecked on this rock of misplaced responsibility.

You can alter this by always asking yourself: "Is this my job, or should someone else be taking responsibility for this?" If the answer is that it's someone else's job but you are doing it, then you must question whether you have created this situation, and change your behaviour.

### Pointlessly competing with everyone else

The third mindset is giving all your power to a competitor in work. When you have developed a successful personal brand that is propelling you forward, you can sabotage yourself if you make competing with others your driving force.

Imagine that you have your dream job in a young, dynamic, growing company and you have a position of influence on the senior management team. You look the part, have mastered projecting a powerful personal brand, have a good personal public relations plan and you are thriving. What could go wrong? You!

If you begin to look around and see others playing office politics and launching a charm offensive on the boss and you internalise your upset at their behaviour, thinking, "they are doing better than me", you will feel disadvantaged, and engage in unfavourable comparisons with others.

What does your attention and energy change to? It's remarkable to watch when someone changes focus to tracking another's manoeuvres and games. You stop looking at your Big Audacious Aim and your milestones. It can distort your whole focus to tracking what they are doing. It does not matter to you that they are on a totally different path. You have just given them all your power. At worst, you become paranoid about the politics going on behind closed doors.

The way to hold power, when you are at a senior level and observing politics, is to hold firm to your plans and to stay focused on what you stand for and what you want to be famous for. This is your own personal brand wedded to your own Big Audacious Aim. If you focus on this you can avoid worrying about others and their activities.

It is self-defeating to concentrate on others and to become influenced by them; if you do, you are not just leaking power, you're a one-person power haemorrhage. Instead, question your own motives and your own insecurities. The real way to blow that sort of thing wide apart is to focus on your job and to dazzle with an unexpected result.

### Setting up your own career limiters

Finally, a further brand-damaging mindset is when you operate from a limiting belief and it becomes a powerful paralyser of your career ambitions. Below are some I have personally come across in the last year – in each case the person was giving all their power away, the limiter was stopping a career dead in its tracks.

This problem of career limiters tends to appear when you are looking for a new job – all the way from the preparation for the job search, through choosing what jobs to apply for, to the interview. It also relates to points of transition for people actually working, like looking for promotion, for assignment to a different department, for inclusion on important new project teams and when there is competition to be assigned overseas.

**"When will I know enough?" syndrome**    The career delimiting can start at the stage of considering if you will apply for a new job or a promotion in your existing company. This is a weakness, particularly for some women, where they have self-confidence issues and feel they do not know enough. They mistakenly believe that more and more qualifications will fill the gap and focus on that instead of just applying and seeing what happens.

I frequently ask women with this hesitant mindset to first follow the following easy steps in a non-judgemental way:
- Look at your CV and look for what you *have to offer* instead of the gaps.
- Look at the job description realistically, and not with a sense of not being up to it.
- Look at your experience and think well of yourself.
- Reach an accurate conclusion; it is very possible that you have the knowledge and the experience needed, that you are being too critical of yourself. In short, you know enough to try for it.
- Then just put yourself forward.

What can you lose? What is the worst that can happen? They don't give it to you. So what? You have improved your interview technique, and they now see you are ambitious. No downside!

Funnily enough, I rarely see this issue with men. They will apply for jobs and tend to move internally more quickly as they don't usually have this inner limiter.

**"I don't have everything they need" syndrome** This is the first cousin of the previous limiter. People read ads for jobs and if they don't have every little thing on the list, they delimit themselves and don't even apply. What they often don't realise is that most of these lists of requirements are wish lists; even the boss does not have all these skills.

**"Thinking of others' interests first" syndrome** Instead of reading the company's needs and then matching your skills, attributes and experience to mirror their requirements, you look at the requirements and decide you can't possibly match them or be good enough: "No need to apply, they will not be able to use me, I can't contribute." Exit stage left even before applying. It might be useful to look at your skills as a separate issue and sell them as something the business needs, even if they haven't thought of it yet.

**"Matching sets of luggage in the interview" syndrome**   I have seen people give away their opportunities because they insist on bringing their personal problems (not just baggage but matching sets of luggage) into a professional interview and ramming them down the interviewer's neck. For example, a woman who had set up her own business, but wanted to get back into the corporate world, viewed her business as a failure so wouldn't talk about it in interviews. In fact, companies viewed it as great experience – she didn't get jobs because it looked like she was hiding something.

**"Letting put-downs define you" syndrome**   I have seen so many excellent people decide to leave a company and as they go they get unsolicited comments from the people who feel left behind. Examples include: "You will have difficulty, seeing as you are so poor with people"; "you will never shine like you did here"; or, a real killer, "you will never find a company like ours who knows how to help you". The comments will always come, and can undermine your confidence in your new role, leading to overcautious behaviour, but don't internalise them or let them delimit you.

**The "nasty comment" syndrome**   Many people feel the need to give you unsolicited feedback on your performance. If the person does not like you, the feedback will be nasty. Remember: unnecessarily negative feedback is all about the giver and not about you. I am surprised by the amount of damage this can do to a person and how it can strip away their power. You can either let it scar you and believe that it is right, or not. The danger is when you internalise a very nasty comment and believe it. For example, at a job interview you may be asked a difficult question and if you have allowed destructive comments to mould your opinion of your own performance, it will delimit you and your answer.

I see perfectly good people rule out whole sectors and companies when planning their future career because of one bad experience of the negative behaviours and comments they received in their current or a previous role: "I won't work for a family business because my last job was with a toxic family – all family businesses are dysfunctional". This may be you overgeneralising.

Below are some sentences encapsulating further limiting beliefs, ones that will leak your power. Do any of them sound familiar? If so, consider the beliefs opposite and how they will help you hold your power.

| Leaking Power Beliefs | Holding Power Beliefs |
|---|---|
| I have to do everything, otherwise it will not be done properly. | Once I have set up the work, I can delegate to people around me and give them clear instructions. |
| I am not good enough, I don't measure up. | I am good at my job, I won't compare myself to others. |
| I need to help everyone, that's the only way they will like me. | I am likeable for who I am, I don't need to be a people-pleaser. |
| I must compete, winning is everything. | I do not have to always compete and I do not have to win everything. I am successful enough to choose when and where I will compete. |
| I am afraid of success, what if I shine too brightly? | I will shine because of who I am and what I do. Shining too brightly is the other person's issue. |
| I am afraid of failure, what will people say if I fall on my face? | I see failure as the way to learn from my mistakes. |
| It's someone else's fault, I only did what was asked of me. | I will take responsibility for everything I do, which will empower me. |
| I always remember the negative aspects – that's how I learn. | I will always balance the negative with the positive. |
| I underestimate resistance; I believe if I order it done, it will be done. | I can get things done, but I will motivate people to do them rather than order them to. |
| I expect too much in the short term, I want it all now. | I will stop being too hard on myself, I will get there but I need to take time. |
| I can't do what I want, others are holding me back. | I am in charge of my own destiny. |

## 2. Leaking power through your behaviours

The second big way to leak power and damage your personal brand is through certain power-leaking behaviours at work; there are many such behaviours, but I have identified six major ones for you.

### Being everyone's friend

**The leak**   The imperative to please people at all costs can mean you leak power to those you appease. It is most striking when, instead of providing direction, setting stretch goals and creating a motivating but results-driven environment, you try to be everyone's understanding friend.

This can happen when you are in charge of a group of people or a number of service providers and you want to be their pal, not their manager. Sounds like the job of any manager, yes, but there are people who are incapable of managing people. They leak all their managing power for reasons like:

- Fear of conflict: they think if they give direction they won't be able to handle push-back from staff.
- Not wanting to be seen as bossy: they don't know how to lead with fairness.
- Having a fundamental need to be liked and affirmed on a constant basis.

**The hold**    Holding power comes from realising that, as a manager, you have a different role. You can be an agreeable person but professionally you are the boss. Your staff are there to help you get the job done and you need to ensure they do. You need to hold people accountable and give them responsibility.

### The illusion of impact

**The leak**    Sweeping into a meeting, full of stories about your personal dramas may look like you are making an impact, but in fact you are dissipating your power. You are projecting two competing signals: I am a professional business person, yet I am also an attention-seeking diva.

I have seen it happen, where someone arrives and tells you all about their journey, their near-miss accident, their parking misadventures, their accident yesterday and, no lie, their dog's health status. The effect is of a shattering piece of glass exploding in front of you. You have given away your chance to make a powerful impression and instead have made a splintered impact.

Now you have to re-orientate the others in the meeting to see you as a serious person: here to sell a product, get a contract, and even persuade them to employ you.

**The hold**    Think about the initial impact you want to make on people, possibly a different impact on different occasions. Decide what you need them to think about you and concentrate on creating that effect. Drop any diva-like performances; leave them to be played out with your friends.

## All over the place

**The leak**  Being brilliant at the specifics of your job but disorganised about integrating your work back into the overall scheme causes you to lose respect.

For example, being consistently behind on reports of your work, missing deadlines, not taking calls, or losing track of time, all get you the personal brand of being unreliable. Time and time again, I come across middle-level managers who are good at their core job, are technically brilliant, but get the reputation of being a nightmare to work with. In a world of over-supply of technically good people, the differentiator for a senior executive can be these behaviours, and you will not be the number one pick.

**The hold**  Don't just be good at your specific job, sharpen up on your administration skills, your interconnections with others and showing that you are adding value – you're not an island.

## Boundary issues

**The leak**  When you have poor boundaries and allow work colleagues too deeply into your personal life, or probe too deeply into theirs, you lose the power of your professional detachment. Gushing confessionals are inappropriate in work because after you have overshared it's too hard to regain your detachment.

Gossiping about colleagues is a boundary issue. Discussing competencies in a professional setting is one thing, speculating on their sleeping habits is another. You will have difficulty getting your power back if you are seen as the source of all the latest hot gossip.

**The hold**  Remember, in work you have to respect personal boundaries and not feel you can get into people's personal lives; once in, it's hard to get back out. (Regarding gossip, a former boss of mine had a hard line on this, with a single rule: if you didn't see it yourself, then you don't know it happened, and you have no right to say it did.)

## Not seeking and getting clarity on your job

**The leak**  Lack of clarity can occur when you are negotiating the details of a new position, either in a new company or just a transfer to a new role in your existing company. Blurring of expectations occurs and you build trouble if you fail to clarify what you are responsible for.

You need to know what, in six months' time, constitutes success in the boss's eyes. If this ambiguity exists, your personal brand will be in difficulty. How can you hold power when you don't know what is expected? I find this more common in owner-managed businesses; the owner may have grown the business, may have a sizeable staff, but still retains a small business mindset. The owner may have no management training and may have difficulty distinguishing between roles.

In these scenarios you must be careful to really check what you are told in interviews in case you are sold an image of a professional company, only to discover it's really a company being run off the 'kitchen table' and subject to the idiosyncrasies of the owner.

**The hold**    You must do everything to clarify what is expected of you before you start; personal brands are damaged when you cannot meet shifting expectations no matter how hard you work. This is especially true of a driven entrepreneur in a family business. The same rules do not seem to apply in family businesses, even huge ones. The family is always deferred to, especially by long-timers. I have seen a number of people crash and burn because they could not handle the family dynamic.

## Losing power under stress

**The leak**    Are you the same person under stress? I have worked with healthcare professionals at management level who work long shifts in a stressful environment. We did a workshop on personal branding, particularly in relation to their leadership of teams. We all got an interesting insight when we had finished crafting their personal brands and included all their aspirations and ideals about what they wanted to project. The acid test came when we did a role play around maintaining their power at the end of a long shift.

It emerged that under stress and when tired they began to leak power and to damage their personal brands. The managers knew they were crankier, less understanding, more demanding that things just be done and they knew they were operating as their lesser selves. The managers recognised that staff around them had observed this, and so had adopted ways to cope, like avoiding them and deferring raising difficult issues. They realised that staff had been complaining about how they were managed at these specific times and that they had been ignoring the complaints.

**The hold**    If this is you, ask yourself: "What am I like when I am under stress? Would I like to be around me then?" The answer lies in your honest realisation that you need to work harder on holding onto your power when you know you are exhausted. Don't ruin a great personal brand by behaving badly because you are tired.

## 3. Leaking power in wicked environments

To me, wicked environments are those that are toxic to you and that render you powerless. They overwhelm you, and totally damage you and your personal brand. I have observed two main ways in which this happens:

- Leaking power to the company set-up.
- Leaking power to poor leadership.

Below I set out my principles for regaining and holding your power. In the case of dealing with poor leadership, I have developed a 'hold your power' strategy which you can use to protect yourself. You will find it later in this step.

### Leaking power to the company set-up

It is possible to find yourself in a work situation that is crippling your personal brand; you are being put into a completely reactive situation and you feel you are no longer in control. This can happen to the best of us and can creep up slowly.

I have worked with people who find themselves in this place and the case study below illustrates how certain companies can prevent you from shining. Before we begin Jack's story, let me say that I marvel at how some companies work out who progresses up the ladder.

### JACK: HOLD POWER AND PLAY TO YOUR STRENGTHS

Jack had joined a major consultancy company at the middle level and was now navigating its elaborate courtship process to get his next promotion.

It seemed to me that you needed to project an equal measure of studied humility and calculated self-promotion to get to the next level. There were induction sessions, internal mentors appointed and much-engineered feedback sessions, but basically you needed to develop a powerful personal brand within months of joining and have excellent relationship-building skills so that you could show-case it to the decision-makers.

This set-up suits people who have narcissistic tendencies, but not Jack, who is a reserved, intelligent and very capable man. He was quickly in difficulty, despite the fact that he was a valuable addition to the company.

Jack was leaking power and very unhappy with the situation in which he found himself. Instead of gaining confidence as he settled in, he was losing confidence and now had less than he'd had five years previously.

After joining, Jack worked on getting new business and, despite the difficult economic climate, succeeded. He was assigned to a particular partner who was to be his guide. This person did not attempt to understand Jack's personality, but offered generalised advice totally unsuited to a reserved person. The partner's advice unnerved and further weakened Jack. He was told to "get out there and make everyone important notice you"; "go meet them and get their advice"; "socialise your case for promotion". In effect, Jack was supposed to simultaneously reach out for advice and impress strangers in a series of contrived short meetings.

Jack found it difficult to approach these important people and when he did so it was as a supplicant asking for advice, not as a confident member of the company. His manner was tentative and unsure. His shyness and desire for privacy were under strain. The whole process of asking for advice, getting feedback and making a case for his promotion simply exhausted his limited reserves of energy.

Jack asked for comments on his performance from people who delivered superficial judgements and then he absorbed them without dispute. He listened too much to personal comments. He was allowing these people take all his power, almost casually. They were not really invested in him and he allowed their words to diminish him.

At the end of three months of this approach he had lost his confidence. It seemed to me that this was like a 'beauty pageant' approach to promotion: superficial and based on little real interaction. This was when I met Jack. He was torn between cutting his losses and leaving, or staying and working the process.

He decided to postpone leaving and to try a new approach. To regain his footing we focused on a plan that would play to his strengths, which were his impressive industry experience, his powerful contacts and his quiet but resourceful approach to getting business. He held his power by leveraging his strengths and working them.

Jack stopped asking for indiscriminate generalised advice and this immediately allowed him to switch to holding his power. We decided that he would only stick to the letter of the law on the company's process, while operating a plan crafted around his personality.

Jack worked on figuring out who the major players were, the major committees and the main criteria used to get promotion. He focused on these and conserved his energy for them. He began making presentations of high content to influential groups; this helped him to regain his energy and rebuild his power. He played to his quiet, detailed, insightful style and did not try to fake an extraverted style. He returned to his authentic self.

If you find yourself in this type of situation, it's best to work the company's process in your own unique way rather than following a generalised formula.

## Leaking power to poor leadership

In the last few years I have seen personal brands suffer the most in situations when someone has to deal with negative leadership behaviours.

In many cases technical experts are promoted on the basis of their expertise, but receive limited management training or development support themselves. They get the job and are left to sink or swim. When this happens, people muddle through and the people side of the business is not being run on the best professional basis. In this vacuum, certain unprofessional behaviours can grow and get out of control. I call these the behaviours of the psycho or bully leader.

### Vincent: Leaking Power to the Psycho Leader

Vincent regularly reported to a management board run by a very difficult man who had psychopathic tendencies. This man initially appeared charming and welcoming when Vincent joined the company, but quickly the mask dropped and the real person appeared. He never listened, picked on people and was constantly on the hunt for people to blame.

This chairman was the schoolyard bully, running around drunk with power. He actually lunged across the table at one meeting and roared at Vincent for allegedly ruining one of his businesses, despite the fact that he was turning it around. I am aware this is a very extreme example, and hopefully you won't come across this type of leader, but the work Vincent did on his personal brand in the face of such negative behaviour convinced me that to make your brand impervious to such attacks is to strengthen it beyond belief.

If anything could be worse than the chairman's behaviour, it was the henchmen and women with whom he surrounded himself. Their job was to mollify the victims of his outbursts, make sure no one directly challenged him and to make the world appear as he needed. This involved a lot of manipulative conversations, coercion, and a good deal of passive-aggressive behaviour directed at Vincent.

Not surprisingly, Vincent began to leak all his power.
- He felt very badly treated and intimidated.
- He began to distrust his own considerable business judgement.
- He could not really promise his staff anything because he might not be able to deliver if the board changed its mind.
- He was exhausted, stressed and fighting to keep his motivation.

The best solution for Vincent was to gather up all his power and quit before he was irreversibly damaged. However, he did not want to go on the job market at a time when he was feeling so unconfident. We had many conversations during his two years in this company and we worked to get him to protect himself and to reclaim his power using the 'hold your power' strategy explained below.

Though Vincent could not change the chairman, using the 'hold your power' strategy grew his ability to protect himself.

If you think you are stalling in your career or just not succeeding as well as you imagine you deserve, then I hope you have recognised one or more of the leaking power examples above. It is one thing to know you are leaking power, but it is important to move quickly to learn how to hold your power. I hope you find that the strategy described below works as well for you as it has for my clients.

## Hold your power strategy

### Holding your power when you face bad leadership behaviours

The issues in cases like Vincent's and Jack's are the bad behaviour of the leader, the lack of any accountability, accompanied by no visible constraint on the excesses from a higher authority.

So, in both cases, Vincent and Jack were on their own and had to find their own solutions or be forced to leave. The answer to taking their power back lay in a four-step approach:
1. Know yourself
2. Understand bad behaviours
3. Develop a strategy to hold your power
4. Detach yourself.

### 1. Know yourself

Vincent and Jack had to learn all about themselves and why they were particularly vulnerable to this form of behaviour. What was it about their personal brand that may have contributed to this?

This is why it is so important to begin the development of your personal brand with a good deal of work on getting to know and understand yourself. If you are unfortunate enough to be in this type of situation, you can use all the work you did in Steps 1 and 2 and apply it here.

The first time someone bullies you, you get a shock and you are a surprised victim. The second time it happens, and you accept it, an unspoken pact is agreed: you have told the bully you accept this behaviour. At the beginning you have been unwittingly targeted, but from the second time on you are aware, you are now willingly compliant in their abuse of power. Remember, bullying is consistently unacceptable behaviour that is repeated over and over again.

So my first piece of advice is never to enter into this unspoken pact. Challenge unacceptable behaviour straight away at the source. Do it professionally and in an adult way.

Vincent worked hard on understanding why he was so susceptible to being dominated in this way and why he had put up with it for so long. Obviously, because his boss was involved, it was more complicated than being bullied by a colleague. He was afraid.

We concluded that Vincent had indeed fallen victim to bullying and had accepted the bad behaviours from the beginning. As he had never called his boss on his unacceptable behaviour, he had let it continue and deteriorate. Recognising that you are being drawn into their cycle of behaviour is a good start.

## 2. Understand the bad behaviours

Vincent needed to totally understand and decode the bad behaviours of the bully so he could detach, observe and protect himself. When he broke down the behaviour into its constituent parts and watched it in a detached way, he was able to see it was not a personal attack, but the chairman's normal behaviour. When he observed that the chairman did this to everyone and in a predictable set of steps, it empowered him and he became expert in seeing the cycle of rage. Vincent saw the triggers: the search for the victim, the rising anger, the rage, the explosion, the uncontrolled rant, the abrupt dismissal.

Three books that are very useful in helping people to recognise bad leadership behaviours are: Jay Carter's *Nasty People: How to Stop Being Hurt by Them without Stooping to Their Level* (McGraw-Hill, 2003), which clearly outlines the behaviours of what he calls 'invalidators', like Vincent's boss. Anyone I have ever given that book to says it is an excellent decoder of the ways in which overly aggressive people or bullying people behave.

Secondly, the whole issue of psychopathic behaviour is well covered by Robert Hare (originator of the Hare test for diagnosing psychopathy) and Paul Babiak in *Snakes in Suits: When Psychopaths Go to Work* (Harper-Business, 2007). Finally, *Office Politics* by Oliver James (Vermillion, 2013) is a great "guide to thriving in a world of lying, backstabbing and dirty tricks". I recommend these to any of my clients who find themselves in situations where they are leaking power to poor leadership behaviours.

The good news is that Vincent successfully survived for two years and did such a good job that he easily got another job and a glowing reference from his antagonist. In the end, Vincent realised his boss had actually respected him because of his handling of the situation.

## 3. Develop a strategy to hold your power

You may recognise this cycle when you work for someone with appalling lack of leadership skills. You join, you work hard, you get criticised, you get invalidated, you begin to defend yourself, you concentrate on escaping their wrath, you become demotivated, you narrow your focus to staying out of trouble, your confidence drops, you doubt yourself, you get depressed, you are very unhappy and you have leaked absolutely all your power.

> A direct quote from Vincent says it all: "The biggest challenge I had was learning not to internalise the other person's dysfunction and to develop the skills to reframe their dysfunction and neutralise its effect on me."

Of course, you must reach out for support within the company and use the services provided by human resources if you are, in fact, being bullied, but even with that support it is worth knowing how to protect yourself from getting sucked into the bully's cycle of behaviour. The reason I am proposing this model to you, and in fact why I developed it in the first place, is because it would be a great shame if, having worked hard to develop a great personal brand, someone could still disempower you and really damage your brand. If you do not develop the skills to cope with these people, you are in career danger.

Have a look at this model of the stages of behaviour of a typical difficult boss and how you could cope with them.

This strategy outlines the steps an aggressor takes while attacking you and the typical victim response. See if you adopt the typical response, then look at the alternative possible responses: that of a non-victim; and the poweful one of mastery, where you hold all your power.

### HOLD YOUR POWER STRATEGY

| Aggressor | Victim behaviour | Non-victim behaviour | Hold your power |
|---|---|---|---|
| Trigger sets him off. Gets upset. Anger builds. | Provide the trigger and mirror emotions. | Be aware of the trigger. Avoid providing them. | Become an expert on what sets the person off. |
| Looks for target, moves on target. Spots target. | Look and feel scared. Draws him onto you. | Avoid contact | You are impervious |

| Aggressor | Victim behaviour | Non-victim behaviour | Hold your power |
|---|---|---|---|
| Slow wind up | Argues | Let it begin. Do not engage. | Stay detached, and observe steps. |
| Rant begins | Self justifies | Stay silent | You now realise that they have given you all their power as they are visibly out of control. |
| Rant continues | Tries to explain | Stay grounded | Ask questions to shift person to rational mindset |
| May get personal. May try to provoke you. | Takes it personally. Gets visibly upset. | Do not take it personally, see this as just another rant. | Radiate detachment and the personal remarks will rebound on them. |
| Rant may go over the top | Encourages by defending self | Control your emotions | Be so beyond remarks that they start to look vindictive |
| Can go on for 2–3 minutes | Takes it all on board | Let it roll, detach and observe | Hold your power. It is not your show |
| Rant ends. Winds down. | Speak and risk setting aggressor off on rant again | Wait for end | Hold the power and resume as if no rant took place |
| Moves on | Stay in victim mode | Stay detached and chart the steps of that rant | Use the fact that the person realises that you are immune to silently deter another one |
| You are dismissed | Leave upset | Leave unaffected | Be professional |

If you find yourself in a similar situation, the following exercise is for you to record what is happening so you can analyse it and see the repeating patterns. I have seen people use this model and transform their personal brand from one of a beaten-down executive to a detached professional, totally in control of themselves. If the above resonates with you and you are in this situation, carry out this exercise.

### HOW TO HOLD YOUR POWER AGAINST BAD LEADERSHIP BEHAVIOURS

| Record the steps of the cycle | Record your usual response behaviour | Decide on your new responses |
|---|---|---|
| | | |
| | | |
| | | |
| | | |
| | | |
| | | |
| | | |
| | | |
| | | |

## 4. Detach yourself

The purpose of using the hold your power model is to move you away from an emotional engagement in the irrational behaviour of another person. You begin to see the predictable phases in the cycle of their rants. Knowing it is never personal – but simply an extreme form of behaviour directed at you because you are there – allows you to detach yourself. It's not about you, it's all about them. What you are seeing is the person's own vulnerabilities playing out in front of you. If you become a master of this model, your personal brand will be safe and theirs will be damaged, not the other way around.

In conclusion, I want you to be aware of the combination of your behaviours, your potential derailers, covered in previous steps, along with the ways you leak power, discussed here. I want you to realise that even when you have worked hard to build a powerful brand, you need to be vigilant and not allow anyone or any environment to take your power. Holding onto your power will be a cornerstone of your sustainable personal brand.

# Step 7

## The playing field for your brand: your matrix

*"Try not to become a man of success but rather try to become a man of value."*

Albert Einstein

® **The matrix**
® **Challenging matrix situations**
® **The art of managing up**
® **Instructive managing up scenarios**

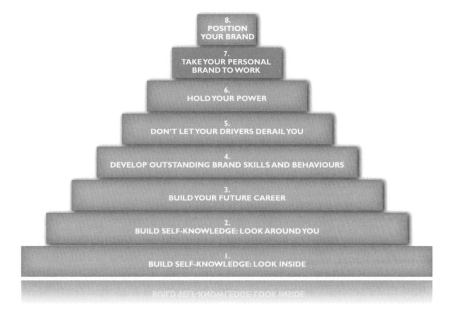

## The matrix

The previous steps cover all the aspects of how you create your personal brand, shape it with your behaviours, protect it from derailing behaviours and finally learn how to hold onto your personal power. Now that you have your personal brand in the best possible shape, the logical next step is to look around you and see where it is regularly on view. This step will introduce you to the concept of carefully looking at your work environment and understanding how to interconnect it with your personal brand. It will be a revelation to you and will embed your personal brand in the reality of your everyday work life.

Most of us work in a complex work structure, be it a national company, multinational or medium-sized business. I call this complex environment your "matrix". It is composed of a big grid of the people above you, your peers and the people who report to you. In some companies it can also include suppliers and customers. In short, it is the complex web of connections that make up your working environment. It is the playing field for your personal brand.

## Mastering the matrix

There are three stages to mastering the matrix:
- Know it
- Map it
- Work it

After those stages you then deal with the specifics of your circumstances. For this I have shared a number of scenarios I have observed, with lessons for you to consider.

### The matrix: know it

Everyone must develop their own matrix; this is one of the most important exercises I engage in with anyone developing a personal brand. A fundamental tool is your diagram of your corporate matrix.

It's a straightforward process. Get a sheet of paper and write out all the names of the people who have any link to you at work: people above, peers, people under you, significant people in major suppliers, outside agencies, partner companies or service providers. You will end up with a sheet full of names. You may need to consult an organisational chart. I find this exercise can be a revelation to some as they had their head so firmly in their silo that they failed to realise how many others have a potential effect on them.

### The matrix: map it

Step one: take those names and make a diagram, putting you in the middle and arranging everyone else around you, above, same level and below. Take a look at this and see how extensive it is.

Step two: this is like a quality audit. Decide if each person supports you, might potentially harm you, or is capable of both. Think back to some of the poor leadership behaviours described earlier and you can see how some of those people would fall into the category of a harmer. Supporters are the people who choose you for key roles, allow you travel to new locations, and are actively interested in your success. Usually when someone is both a harmer and a supporter, there is a good deal of their ego at play.

Step three: check the last time you had a meaningful interaction with each of them. In the case of supporters, prioritise some meaningful interaction with them. That could be a meeting, asking to be part of an initiative they are leading, volunteering for something they are involved in, asking if they would mentor you or just asking for advice. Use your imagination; the main point is to get out of your comfort zone and be visible to people you need to notice you.

If you have noted someone as a harmer, then make sure you do not run afoul of them. If they are toxic, avoid them, but do not get on their wrong side. Again, refer to previous steps for strategies to help you. If someone is both a supporter and a harmer, then pay extra care to every interaction with them. An example could be a very well-connected senior executive, two levels up from you, who has the power to get you assigned to challenging but visible projects which will raise your profile, thereby supporting you. But perhaps that person is also very egotistical and, if he perceives you as having crossed him personally, will use his well-connected position to say unflattering things about you to key people and harm your career.

### The matrix: work it

If you are actively seeking promotion, transfer or to get involved in more cross-functional work, this matrix map works like a dream. I encourage people to make a plan over a number of months to systematically work their way around all the important people on their matrix.

Dorothy was working for a manipulative director, Michael, who was well known as a wrecker of the career of anyone who got in his way. He was known to take delight in nasty gossip and malicious joy at another's discomfort; he was engulfed with Schadenfreude when he saw people get into difficulty.

Dorothy liked her job, loved the company and hated Michael in equal measure. We began with her matrix and made a plan for her to work around Michael to build an independent personal brand with people across the company. She had an excellent mind and could provide useful business knowledge to heads of operations in other countries. Dorothy did this very well, and Michael began to hear great praise for her. He might have still tried to wreck her personal brand but was astute enough to realise he would not be believed, so he backed off.

## Making an impression on your matrix

I hope by now you'll agree that it's a myth that being good at your job alone gets you promoted. Today it is increasingly difficult to actually quantify a person's outputs. When you could count the widgets produced or units sold, you had something quantifiable. Today, it's all about service – outputs and adding value are more elusive.

This contributes to the trend of depending on your perception of how well a person is doing, your view of their positioning and of course their personal brand in your judgement of someone. Increasingly there is reliance on the leader's intuition for picking and developing winners. In his international bestseller *Thinking, Fast and Slow* (Penguin Books, 2012), Daniel Kahneman shows how flawed intuition really is, and how we often replace making a hard decision with making an easier one without noticing the substitution.

You need to think about the impression you are making on others in your matrix and to look around you to see the reality so you can adapt to it. You must notice when you make a good impression or annoy your colleagues, be aware of your effect on customers, realise how your team behave around you. People who easily adapt to what is going on around them have the advantage: they tend to be more flexible and read what is expected of them and behave accordingly. It's the triumph of the chameleons.

Take this into the context of any workplace and look around you. Your success depends largely on your ability to read the people around you and the adaptive strategies you develop.

## Be proactive in matrix management

*It's not the elevator pitch that's important; it's who you're in the elevator with*! It would be foolish to be naïve about successful people who move up the career ladder and their intentions towards you. The more senior people become, the more astute they are at managing the matrix. As I said earlier, ability alone does not get you promoted. You can be a legend in your own mind, but if the right people don't notice, you will remain famous only in your own mind.

I sometimes meet people who say that they think office politics is fake and they don't want any part of it. But that's a foolish conclusion if you want to succeed in any large organisation. It is not hard to spot the over-confident, under-talented colleagues who have manoeuvred their way to the top, just look around you.

## Don't forget the important customers

Whether you work for a multinational, professional services firm or SME, your internal and external customers are a hugely important part of your matrix.

Just because you're out of the office, it doesn't mean that your personal brand is not being reported back in. Beware the inner circles at the top of the corporate world. If you go off-site to carry out a major audit and behave badly, it will be known. If you fail to read the client right and just annoy them, it will get back to those above you.

Take Deborah, who was in danger of being let go because she simply could not get along with the company's main client. Her job was to liaise with the client, help define what was needed, provide it and, above all, manage the client's potent mix of insecurity and aggressiveness. It was a case for careful reading of the person, adaptive strategies and a huge amount of burying one's ego, while stroking the client's. Instead, Deborah decided she was going to behave as she always did, got miffed by the client, let her own ego get in the way and ended up alienating the client.

The complaints back were all personal and highly toxic, ranging from "I cannot work with her" to "I'll change the account to another company if you don't remove her". She was taken off the account and put elsewhere; her personal brand is still in recovery.

It also works in reverse: if you are the client from hell, word gets around all the suppliers, who now badmouth you around their industry.

## Essential matrix actions for success

### Staying in the loop

With many of my clients, one of the most common areas for development noted in their annual appraisals is the need for them to understand more aspects of the business they are in, and to show more commercial acumen. I find specialised people often ignore other sections of their company:

- Accountants can fail to understand the actual products and services of the company.
- Marketing people can too often not stay abreast of business-critical financial information.
- People in head office often fail to understand the reality of major suppliers or vendor networks.

Your personal brand is damaged if you are seen to be unaware of key areas of your business; you get the reputation of having a narrow focus and perhaps of being someone who lives in a silo in the business.

Develop business intelligence; quite a lot of information about your sector can be gained from external sources, market and industry commentators. Reading all information coming from the press and communications sections is useful.

As most people like to stay in their comfort zones, you immediately stand out if you work at understanding all sides of the company. Make a list of the aspects of your business that you know the least about, then do something about it.

This is an easy one to fix and will make it much easier to have meaningful interactions across the different parts of your matrix.

### Get a sponsor

One of the best ways to navigate the matrix is to get a sponsor within the company. Ideally, this is a senior figure. It's best if they are a few layers up, as someone just above you may see you as a rival – go far enough up so you are no threat.

Elder lemons love being asked for advice and being known for fostering brilliant new talent. Rather than being awestruck by them, pay them the compliment of asking for advice and guidance. If they like you, they can become a full sponsor and greatly help your career. Is that not the whole basis of the television show *The Apprentice*?

## Challenging matrix situations

There are many instances where the matrix within an organisation can impact your personal brand and your career. I hope that by reading the following, all based on a compendium of real examples, you will get a sense of what I am talking about.

## 1. What if you parachute into a company at a senior level?

*The dilemma*

There was a time when people in companies followed a lifelong career and rose slowly and steadily to the top. I remember my first job was in the Department of Finance, where I entered as a graduate at the Administrative Officer level. It was a rigorous entry process based on stiff competition, with many obstacles, including proficiency in Irish. When I entered I realised that the expectation was that if you were lucky enough to get in, you were in for life!

The next grade up was Assistant Principal, a lofty position at the time. About 30 of us entered over a two-year period and our favourite pastime was discussing the people at the top of the list for promotion. There was a system based on 'first in, first promoted'. A glut of us, lots of new blood, had joined a static system, so our chances of promotion really came down to one of the APs falling under a bus so we could all move up one level. The idea of anyone parachuting in over our heads was alien. I lasted four years.

Sadly, there are still some companies in Ireland where there are a lot of people who entered a system like that and know no other. Commercial realities, deregulation and privatisation have changed the game, and companies now want to bring in highly-qualified experts to perform key functions to modernise and build profitability.

These people do drop in out of the sky. If you are one of these, you will be acutely aware of the problems of having no "previous" in a company of long-established people. Usually these people enter at a critically high level with an agenda of change.

Most important is the little-understood role of informal leaders in a matrix. These are the people who lurk in the long grass, take no official responsibility, but are key influencers of opinion. Lose them and you are over. While not openly conflicting with you they will, if provoked by you, work in the background to sabotage your personal brand and use key phrases like:

- "Who does he think he is?"
- "We were fine before she came."
- "What does he know about our company?"
- "She is only in it for the money."
- "He does not understand our culture."

All these remarks are designed to undermine you, define you as an outsider and weaken your position.

### The strategy

Building a personal brand in this matrix is a real challenge. Unlike all the long-term people around you, who have built up long-lasting relationships and know who to trust, you are walking in blind. You are at a distinct disadvantage, and to succeed you need to understand your matrix and build strong relationships with key players fast.

You not only need to understand your matrix, you also need to strengthen the connections, as you will need powerful allies to push through the changes you have been employed to lead. Most people make the mistake of only trying to impress those with 'legitimate power', i.e. C-suite executives or the management team. The 'silent power' could be with someone else entirely: a respected project manager, an IT person or a cleaner who has worked there 30 years. It's important to recognise that your brand needs to be tailored and directed at people who matter, irrespective of title. You can't be seen to be trying overtly to impress only important people, but you should make an effort to interact authentically with all levels until you know the culture and set-up.

## 2. What if you interviewed for the job but someone was promoted in above you?

### The dilemma

What do you do if you interview for a job but you don't get it? What do you do if you think you were the perfect candidate, but suspect something other than competence swung the decision?

Increasingly, as companies contract their workforces and someone leaves as head of a section, the company asks two people at the lower level, often working side-by-side, to compete for a job. Inevitably, one is disappointed and ends up working for their former desk mate. But what if you, the internal candidate, do not get the job, and an external candidate parachutes in over you instead?

I have seen both scenarios and it is a real challenge to manage up in this scenario. Your personal brand has been damaged as you are seen as the one who failed and now you have to prove yourself anew with a boss who, unless he/she is a saint, is looking at you as a competitor.

The biggest challenge is when you sense that the newly promoted person is lacking confidence; it's one thing to get a job, another to do it.

What do you do when you know they need your expertise, system knowledge, customer knowledge and relationships with buyers, dealers, sales force, and you feel disinclined to share it with them? I have often seen people handle this by retreating into a childlike resentment and watch as all their toys come flying out of the cot.

## The strategy

This is a real challenge for you! You need to map out a strategy where both of you preserve your personal brands. Successful and emotionally intelligent management of this difficult situation can mark you out. I have seen one person who was the head of the Human Resources department, but then her company changed the organisational structure and created a position above her and called it "Director of HR". She was invited to apply for the position, did not get it and watched as an outsider came in and took over the position. Initially she was very disappointed and resentful, but she survived and indeed triumphed because, after much discussion and reflection, she decided on a set of principles to guide her through. These principles enabled her to remain professional and to avoid bringing too much emotion into work.

They were to:
- remind herself daily that what had happened was not personal, so she could maintain professional detachment;
- put herself in the other person's mindset and see things from their point of view;
- focus on the actual things she was being asked to do and resisting colouring them with emotional associations;
- use open and courteous body language;
- be professional and gracious at all times;
- get over it and move on. It was not a personal tragedy.

She didn't realise that her behaviour was being keenly observed by very senior people, and they were greatly impressed by her handling of the situation. Her professional maturity was noted and her personal brand not only recovered but improved.

## 3. What if you back a falling star, thinking it's a rising one?

### The dilemma

As you look at your matrix be careful who you choose to align with. It is inevitable that you will like some colleagues more than others, but there is a danger in becoming too closely identified with one person.

## CLAIRE: DON'T BACK A FALLING STAR

Claire was recruited, on her return from working in New York, into an insurance institution. She came with a prestigious personal brand and was welcomed as a vibrant addition to the firm. She was to work under the direction of a senior partner and to set up a new division of the company offering a new set of services. Together they were billed as the shiny new division, the trend-setters. The senior partner seemed to be the rising star of the company, and she would shine with him. She worked hard and progressed the project through the planning, pilot and launch stages and continued to be seen as a promising addition to the firm.

Claire was focused on the project, worked hard and delivered. Not once did she look above and around her at her matrix. She barely noticed when another young man, Mark, similar to herself, joined a year after her. She did not notice his excellent networking skills, his naked ambition or his superlative matrix management.

As she worked on the project she became increasingly close to her senior partner, often lunching with him on their own. What she did not realise was that the younger partners wanted to sideline the senior partner, and to take the company in a different direction.

As Claire spent more and more time with this partner, the younger partners classified her as "his" person and loyal only to him. Meanwhile, Mark was aligning himself with all the other partners, building a personal brand as the super-confident deal maker.

A perfect storm composed of separate but interconnecting elements – Claire's isolation, her head-down approach, her identification with the no-longer-rising star, and her lack of matrix management – all combined to destroy her personal brand and her position in the company.

The younger partners backed a new scheme positioned by Mark as an alternative to her partner's one. Resources were diverted, her partner was sidelined, ultimately to take early retirement, and Mark was promoted, becoming her new boss.

Was he better than her? No. Was he a better master of the matrix? Yes.

### The strategy

You need to keep your eyes open all the time and to be aware of the political manoeuvrings above you. Keep all your options open and network widely, building alliances across the company. Never become too aligned with any one person, and never be seen as anyone's favourite.

You know the saying "keep your friends close but your enemies closer". Now you have to have a strategy for where you keep your frenemies. A 'frenemy' is a mixture of friend and enemy: someone who is friendly, but who is out to get you, as they see you as a rival.

They can be the people in your matrix who smile at you as they stick the knife in. You need to be quick at spotting them and know how much you can trust them. It's important to realise that frenemies might change according to the context. In one situation they might see you as a rival, but in another they may have a more benign view of you.

### Summary

The moral of the story is that in no case was the actual competence of the person the prime consideration; it was all about the matrix they were working in, the Machiavellian strategies and their own ability to navigate through these things.

## The art of managing up

Managing your people is an entry-level requirement for promotion; there are many courses on managing people, usually meaning managing down, but precious few on "managing up". You need to get good at managing up to navigate a matrix, and to get through the thicket of senior management.

#### PETER: MATRIX MANAGEMENT EXPERT

I worked with a remarkable man who was the best I have ever seen at matrix management. Peter worked in leading change management programmes all across an expanding multinational company. He had no boss and yet he had every divisional director as his "boss". He was only as good as his last successful programme, and he was constantly selling himself and his team to internal customers. If no one was asking him to lead one of their change programmes, his job was in danger.

Peter knew this and so he developed a wondrous and ever-changing matrix map as his main tool for success. He was on top of all developments at head office, knew all the major players internationally and knew what they liked and disliked. He knew that his career and his teams depended on his making this a core activity of his daily routine.

His strategies to positively influence his main targets included:
- Developing and sharing insightful business analysis.
- Bringing people together who were useful to each other.
- Becoming an avid student of psychology to enhance his understanding of people.
- Relentless attention to detail and making excellence his default norm.
- Volunteering to organise the schedules of all visiting senior leaders.
- Knowing everyone's birthday, spouse's name, children's names, special interests.
- Knowing special requirements and providing them unasked.

Peter succeeded extremely well, but we spotted one gap. He was operating in only two divisions of the business, but the business was growing across five divisions. Key influencers were emerging and he needed to look for and deliver programmes that would catch the attention of these new groups.

He also knew that he had to get publicly recognised, as this would get him traction with the highly image-driven top executives. They would want to be associated with a recognised high flyer. Peter was sharp enough to know that winning this recognition was an election campaign, done invisibly but systematically. None of this would have happened if he had not been a stellar performer, but again, he knew that this alone was not enough.

I was very pleased when he won an industry award and was widely praised for that. A perfect piece of matrix management!

## Instructive managing-up scenarios

A key aspect of managing up is learning how to observe accurately and then take the appropriate action. It is not about blundering about, hoping for the best! I would say there is an art to managing up, as the following challenging stories show. I chose two of the most difficult types of boss, as there are great lessons to be learnt from them.

## Managing the 'me, myself and I' boss

Marie is a dynamic, late-30s ball of energy backed up by a fierce intelligence. You know when she enters a room, impeccably dressed, well groomed and sparkling with fun. She has excellent relationship skills and business savvy. In short, you would hire her tomorrow and when you realised what she can do, you would do everything to hang onto that level of talent. You would, that is, unless you were a highly ambitious boss intent on working the system to get yourself promoted to the next level.

### MARIE: MANAGE YOUR BOSS'S PERCEPTION OF YOU

Marie was getting very frustrated in her job and burning out. She had delivered on all her key performance indicators, exceeded in some. She was in charge of a business-critical function, but was being slowed down by a poor performing colleague whose input she needed for her work. Her boss promised her she would have steady growth in responsibility and that when the next vacancy arose, she would be promoted into it.

So, on that promise Marie worked her hardest and delivered dazzling results. When the expected vacancy arose, she began planning what she would do in her new role. Imagine her surprise on a Monday morning to be told that the poor performer had just been promoted and she had not. She was shocked and felt betrayed. Marie's boss could not explain his actions, and began to behave like an angry ostrich: head in the sand, tail feathers all ruffled!

Our analysis of the situation was that Marie's boss had figured that he had one more year in his position before he would be transferred to another division (the policy of the organisation was to rotate high-potential people around the different divisions as a way of preparing them for entry to the top levels). He knew Marie would bring huge reforming zeal to the job and cause him lots of challenges as she tried to change things. He chose the plodder, because he would not cause waves and he could keep Marie focused on her area, delivering and making him look good.

Marie's boss had crafted a situation where his reports delivered and made no waves, so he could coast to his new promotion. Ultimately, he had chosen to make himself look good and to match the system's perception of success. This was just the way it worked – good leadership and loyalty were clearly an unnecessary, optional extra.

Were we being paranoid? I don't think so. The company culture was based on graduates joining after college, working in this large but benign atmosphere. Once in, you were there for life and you progressed along rigid pathways. Marie's challenge was she had been brought in from outside as the company tried to face up to the new world of deregulation. She was like a desert island in this structure.

Marie was being sacrificed on the altar of her boss's clever use of the old system and his total focus on making his transition to the next level as smooth as possible. His focus was on his career, the organisation came second and his team a poor third. Was he selfish or was he a product of 20 years' indoctrination in how to work the system?

Needless to say, Marie is now actively looking outside as she knows she will not succeed in this culture and she realises that when her boss predictably rotates, he will be replaced by another ambitious lifer. The lesson is that one shining outsider in a key role does not a reformed organisation make. Either you change the rules to allow your new talent to flourish as equally as the old guard, or you merely set up a system where the new talent comes in and rotates out after a short number of years.

The lesson is to carefully scrutinise the matrix and see if you can build widespread alliances. Here's some simple wisdom: don't always believe your boss's promises, they're not worth the paper they're not written on.

## Managing an incompetent boss

It happens; your boss leaves and they appoint someone who is good at interviews and then they arrive – and you quickly realise that was their one gift. You watch the honeymoon period and say, "She'll settle in", or, "They wouldn't have hired her if she couldn't do the job". Then you begin to realise that no, she is not up to the job, and now you and your personal brand are in jeopardy.

People who are out of their depth and can't perform at their level of management clutch at the nearest life buoy, usually some aspect of the detail of work that they know well. They begin to operate at a level lower than their pay grade: your level. They begin to do your job as they can't do theirs and must be seen to do *something*. They begin to meddle, and in order to prove they are adding value they begin to criticise your work, so that they can be seen to be improving it. You know the 'white knight' syndrome: riding in to save the day, only they wrecked it in the first place.

It is a big challenge to your personal brand when they begin to suggest that you are not good enough, that they have had to step in and fix things for you. Now take it up a level: what can be more damaging than when they begin to criticise you in a larger forum, again so they look like a saviour? Then they decide that really your job is not that important, and can be done with fewer resources. Suddenly you find your support staff is being let go, yet you are expected to deliver the same results.

The lesson is that this is when you have to work the wider matrix and go around the person and make sure you sell your case to the other decision-makers. Yet you have to do that without openly criticising the new boss, as this is a reflection on their staff choices.

I have worked with people in this situation, and those who have a wide and well-developed matrix, who are clearly aware of their talents and contribution, survive better. Anyone who is isolated and working in a silo, with no collaboration with others across the company at a higher level, struggles more.

## Never take a "widow maker" position

A final word of caution about your matrix: never take a position that has ruined a couple of careers before you, especially if the former people were really good. You know it was the position and not the people. I learnt this from reading Peter Drucker, who wrote that the term "widow maker" was used in the nineteenth century in New England to describe a well-built ship that had two fatal accidents in a row. The shipbuilders did not attempt to fix the ship, they broke it up and built a new one.

A position in an organisation that defeats two good people in a row is a "widow maker". No matter how good you are, the odds are stacked against you succeeding. It would be better to break up the position and start fresh. Don't accept a widow maker position!

The conclusion to this step is that there is little point in developing a stunning personal brand in isolation from the company matrix in which you work. I'll leave you with Louis V. Gerstner, Jr. the former CEO of IBM, who said: "The thing I have learned at IBM is that culture is everything."

Next we will look at how you move to the next level and begin to actively position your personal brand.

# Step 8

## Positioning your brand
## for the future

*"Do not go where the path may lead, go instead where there is
no path and leave a trail."*

Ralph Waldo Emerson

® **Positioning your personal brand**
® **Positioning strategies**
® **From positioning to sparkling**

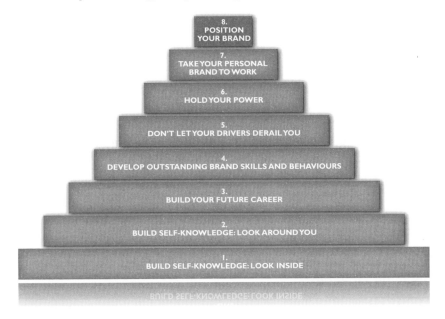

## Positioning your personal brand

At this point in building your personal brand you now know how to
understand yourself, to plan your career, to build outstanding behaviours, to watch for what drives you and see if it can be a derailer, to
hold your power and to work your matrix. The next and final step is
the concept of actively positioning your personal brand to really shine
and be recognised as a stand-out person.

I want to make a strong case to you that all the previous work on building your personal brand will not achieve the outstanding result you require if you don't spend time on building a plan to position yourself. You do not want to be just a legend in your own mind.

## Principles of positioning

### Make a basic proactive positioning plan

Before you scale the heights of stardom, you need to cover the basics. This starts with discovering the best places to stand out and showcase your talents. Look around you in your workplace and see where you can position yourself to be noticed. I know this seems obvious, but I am amazed at the number of people who do not take this basic action.

### The absolute basics

In work, raise your head and seek every opportunity to go beyond merely participating at meetings to:
- chair meetings;
- present findings or plans;
- host conference calls;
- ask good questions at large meetings of all staff.

### The next level

The next level involves moving outside the comfort zone of your known associates and putting yourself forward to:
- Speak at company conferences.
- Become a spokesperson for your group.

It is a little like working your matrix, but the difference here is that you are actively seeking to go beyond being noticed to actively seeking to impress.

### Shine on LinkedIn

If you are not on LinkedIn now, you need to be. It is the simplest and most effective way to position your brand in front of the people you want to impress. It is the essence of a brand positioning tool and must be a core part of your positioning strategy. This is your window to potential employers and head-hunters.

You must create a comprehensive profile and pay attention to all the categories. Don't be fooled into thinking you need large numbers of contacts; I would focus instead on building a solid range of good quality contacts, known personally to you.

You will be able to use a lot of the work you have done while reading this book. For example, you can use your personal brand statement that you developed in Step 2 as part of your profile. All of your insights gained in developing your Big Audacious Aim in Step 3 will be of use in deciding which groups to join and to follow.

## Five positioning principles

I see five different principles you need to position your brand:

### 1. The halo and horns effects

The 'halo effect' is the tendency to attribute positive qualities to a person – or not to notice the negatives – because you like them. It's a good name for a common bias that plays a large role in shaping our view of people and situations. The halo effect increases the effect of first impressions, sometimes to the point that subsequent information is mostly wasted. Quite simply, if you make a very good speech, people can decide you are a high flyer on the halo effect of that alone – they don't actually know anything else about your work. However, there is a double-edged sword at play here because the 'horns effect' also operates. That is, falsely attributing negative qualities to someone because you don't like them. Beware of both when you decide to stand out.

If you position yourself to perform, make sure you are bloody good or you will crash and burn very publicly. (I wonder if it's the fear of this that stops people from seizing this chance to be seen and to showcase their talents.) I see this effect at its most intense when the top brass come to your workplace, from headquarters elsewhere or on a fly-through by the senior management from overseas. In a large organisation, this may be the only chance you have to shine in front of these career makers; it is your 10 minutes of fame.

### 2. The silo principle

Ask yourself these questions: do I have a thriving network? Do I prioritise building connections both inside and outside my company?

**Escape internal silos**   Increasingly, I notice a strange contradiction: the bigger the company, the greater the tendency to live in your safe silo, with the people you believe think like you and speak the same language. There is a huge opportunity to network all across the company, but people just don't.

I recently gave a one-day workshop to 80 middle managers in a large company and it was the first time many of the participants had met in person. They knew each other by name or had phone relationships, but had not thought to walk across the grounds to meet the other person. I am not talking long lunches, just a *hello and how are you?* You are missing a real opportunity to position yourself if you don't reach out.

**Build external networks**   I find many people who work in large corporations neglect to network outside their own company. They seem to feel secure in the big matrix of the company and do not venture out. I can't tell you how many executives fail to return calls or ignore contact from an outsider. It leads to a sort of corporate superiority or closed inwardness. The opportunity to position on a bigger stage is lost. This can be a huge disadvantage and a reality shock when someone like that decides to leave the corporate cocoon or, worse, is made redundant. You can quickly discover that you are only a legend in one sphere, unknown outside.

That means you have to start all over again building connections, you are at a distinct disadvantage compared to others who have a track record in positioning themselves all across the industry.

**Join external associations**   I encourage joining industry or professional associations to broaden your connection base. A word to female executives here: men are far ahead on this because of their traditional involvement in sporting organisations. Women would benefit from more networking. Make it a must to be in at least one external network related to your industry. For a real impact, join a second one.

To really position yourself, you must become active. It is not enough to go to the events: join a committee, make a presentation, organise an event for them. Once you are established, look for ways to deepen your contacts. See if your company can sponsor one of their events, or have one of your bosses speak at it. Think imaginatively, show openness and reach out, you will be pleased with the amount of payback and positive meaningful exposure you will receive.

Remember Adam from the beginning of the book? He would have benefitted from a broader network in the company as he could have checked with people in Asia before he even set foot there. He could have researched the success of similar initiatives in other regions. If he had a large external group of colleagues, he would have minimised his danger of isolation and had a source of informal help and support.

### 3.  The benchmark effect

The 'benchmark effect' is when you know what the global best standard is in your field and you benchmark your performance against that standard. You know the person, company or group that is the world leader in what you do and you keep abreast of their developments. You follow their blogs, tweets, read their books, go see them talk, read about them in business media. You know what the best is and you make that the standard for you to match.

Every year I make the trek to the National Speakers Association annual convention in the United States to see the best speakers in the world and to find out the latest trends in public speaking. I find it a fantastic way to benchmark myself against the best in the world. When did you last benchmark yourself? Are you aware of the latest trends in your sector? Do you know what international person or company is the best at what they do?

I am taken aback at how many people do not know who is the global best in their business. Again and again I ask this question, to be greeted by a blank stare. So, if you find out who the best is, then use that as your benchmark and you will definitely stand out.

This dedication to being the best and to making excellence a hallmark of your work is a powerful positioning tool. You have set your bar at the highest level and when you connect that to networking you are now placing yourself as someone on top of the latest developments, a sure way to be asked to contribute to external events.

External referencing is vital in every company, but especially if you work in a company that thinks they are the best. There is a danger that you will become cut-off and isolated in your own comfort circle. No one company is the best at everything, that belief can lead to arrogance and complacency. So if you are in a company that thinks it's the best and, by extension, you think you are the best, beware!

I would like to alert you to an allied circumstance where you can really position yourself in a bad light. If you are someone with the power to grant contracts to suppliers or outsourced companies, you must not let this position give you unfounded confidence. I have noticed instances where, if you combine the mindset of thinking your company is the best with having a position of power, you can begin to think you are indeed very powerful and positioned at the top of the pile. I have seen executives think they are the best, based on the power they have over suppliers. They are often feared because of their power to end a contract, but not respected for their actual expertise or behaviours.

If we believe that no one is going to stay in any one company for life, then you have to think about if and when you leave and enter the outside world. Over the years, I have observed people regret the position they had engineered themselves into.

### 4. The lifelong learning principle

To position your personal brand and yourself as someone to be rewarded, promoted or head-hunted, you need to be continuously learning and growing your credentials.

I see executives who have gained their initial qualification and then rest happily on that. They justify it by saying they are gaining practical experience while ignoring the fact that they are cutting themselves off from the latest cutting-edge developments. Are you one of them? The acid test for you is to ask yourself when you last undertook a learning programme. If it's been a few years, it's time to take action.

Many people were promoted rapidly in Ireland during the Celtic Tiger years and found themselves operating at the edge of their expertise and running to keep up. They said they were too busy to give time to continuous education. Are you in that situation? If so, you may be positioning your personal brand as one of not staying current.

Anyone who can demonstrate that they are developing their skills, learning more and more industry knowledge, especially analysis of trends and latest developments, stands out from the 'just knowing enough to do the job' person.

Are you thinking of your next job? Maybe in your present job you know enough, but if you wanted to move on, you would find yourself missing some vital qualifications. I have seen a number of instances where people failed to get jobs because the head-hunter found that they did not tick all the prerequisite qualification boxes. Have you ticked all the boxes for your next job?

You need to have an annual self-development budget. This is a crucial step to making you stand out in your career. You need to be knocking down your manager's door looking for support for ongoing education.

## 5. The evolving brand principle

The 'evolving brand' occurs as you progress up the corporate ladder, your personal brand also progresses and you need to reflect these changes in where you position your personal brand.

Let me explain by telling you the following story about an executive who evolved from working with small client accounts to big client accounts. Her personal brand evolved and she had to act accordingly.

She built her professional reputation as a remarkable facilitator, leading focus groups that delivered insightful and useable results. As she grew in her career, she built on her considerable ground-level experience and had progressed to a much higher level, and was now known for her development of campaigns. She had done her long years as a marketer and so her work was excellent, as it was grounded in her years of ground-level experience. This combination of experience and her really imaginative approach marked her out.

Now the dilemma of personal brand evolution emerged because she was still the very best at the ground-level work but had evolved beyond it. Could she be two people: a serious campaign developer influencing boards of companies to innovate and allocate considerable sums of money and human resources to her strategies, and also a facilitator of individual focus groups at the ground level?

I posed this question to her: what if the CEO's spouse came to your focus group and reported back that she had met a lovely woman who ran the group, and then the CEO realised that this was the woman who had influenced his board that morning to spend €5 million? She had evolved and ran the real risk of damaging her personal brand if she did not see how her personal brand had evolved and that she now had to act in a different way.

# Positioning strategies

I am sure you have your heroes, people you look up to because of who they are or what they do. There is something about them that pulls you in and makes you either admire them or want to be a little bit like them. In personal branding terms, if we go full circle to the beginning of this book, they have caused you to have an emotional engagement with them. They have positioned their personal brand in a very strategic way.

Once you have covered the basics of positioning and taken the five effects into account, you then need to work out your own unique positioning strategy. You need to take into account all the work you have done in earlier steps, and – knowing your unique strengths and the impact you want to make – you are now looking for a strategy to go the final furlong.

I would like to share a number of strategies that I have seen work for people.

## I. Be a Charismatic Leader

We already noted earlier that not all bosses are leaders, and now we can add that not all leaders are charismatic. Being good at office politics and positioning yourself is vital. However, a more profound strategy is when you are known as a charismatic leader. This is when you come across with the kind of leadership where charm, personality and 'please follow me' qualities are clearly evident.

### MALCOLM: BE YOURSELF

I came across this situation when working with a senior team preparing for an employee conference at a particularly sensitive time in the company's recovery.

The minimum message the new CEO, Malcolm, had to deliver was to tell the troops the situation and ask for their agreement to all the changes about to be introduced across the company. It was the "I am the new guy on the block and we are going to change the corporate landscape" speech. He had the position, his personal brand as CEO was intact and he could easily have done this. In fact, that was what his senior team was urging him to do. The challenge for him was not to impart the news or to act the CEO. He already had the job! He was going to restructure, whatever happened.

Yet this man was different. He wanted to do more and he was rightly concerned that his speech and his performance had to be just right. He instinctively knew that the employees were a very cynical workforce who thought that they were being put through yet another change programme and that they were wary.

Malcolm was, in fact, a charming man and he genuinely cared. He was also very shy and he knew his challenge was for them to see him as a real person, to let them know he understood how difficult their position was and how he was going to act honourably and protect as many jobs as he could. He had to appear like a real person, one they could relate to and believe in.

We started discussing what Malcolm wanted the audience to think and do when he had finished speaking. After much discussion, he said he concluded that he wanted them to believe he was telling the truth, to feel energised and to believe he cared.

Not surprisingly, giving them a lot of data or a prepared corporate speech would not get him what he wanted. He was going to have to change his whole approach: he was not making a speech; he was going to open a conversation with them.

He told them about himself, he opened up with stories, he showed them he really cared with personal references to his working life. Malcolm really let his engaging and likeable personality show through. He was also brutally honest with them about where the company found itself, and they appreciated his honesty. The feedback he received mentioned that he was a 'no bullshit' person. He had to introduce change, but it was a real person doing this, not some corporate drop-in.

The employees suddenly believed that they had gotten themselves a charismatic leader.

## 2. Be a thought leader

You can work very hard to position yourself as an expert, and many people build personal brands in a particular field, but unless you are very specialised there are always other experts. So if you want to really take a stand-out position for your personal brand, I recommend that you claim the thought leadership space. By 'thought leadership' I mean being the person who is so on top of their game that they become predictors of future trends, they challenge accepted beliefs and practices, they showcase their innovations and they lead thinking on the subject. To do so, they often have to go against common thought and so make some people uncomfortable. Being challenged to think differently moves you outside your comfort zone, and people remember that.

A colleague of mine has become a real thought leader in the area of customer loyalty. She had positioned herself as an expert and had many significant clients working with her. She wanted to progress to the next stage of her personal brand. She crafted a thought-provoking speech and she secured the opportunity to give a series of speeches for a national organisation all around Ireland. She challenged her audiences' thinking, pushed them to drop old views and showcased her innovative approach with great stories.

She capitalised on her position and her speeches moved her personal brand up to a whole new level to thought leader. She went one step further and built on her position as a commentator in publications to actually publishing her own magazine, again moving to thought leader position.

## 3. Leave a legacy

I remember giving a speech to a group of business people on leaving a legacy. I have thought long and hard about this, because earlier in my career I spent time building organisations – particularly their funding base. I was always struck by the difference between a true philanthropist and a narcissistic giver: the philanthropist wanted to make a genuine difference with personal recognition as an optional extra; the narcissist was all about getting recognition. I was also influenced by the number of truly inspirational people who gave freely and abundantly of their time to help build a voluntary organisation from the base up.

In my dealings with American charities I was struck by how some American corporations include an employee's altruistic endeavours in their assessment of their career progress. They were expected to give back and would be rewarded in their career for doing so.

So here is a mind shift that will really set you apart: the decision to build something that will last after you are gone. I don't mean something astonishing, like building a foundation such as the Bill and Melinda Gates Foundation, I mean going to the core of their decision to use their (considerable) resources to make a visible difference in specific areas. For you, it could be when you decide in your career to make giving and making a difference an integral part of your personal brand. This decision can happen at any point in your career, but I think the earlier the better.

This led me to believe that this extra dimension of being a giver and leaving something behind you at different stages of your career made you remarkable. I need to be clear that I don't just mean doing something for charity, that is good, but I also mean making a visible difference in your workplace. I have seen individuals who champion change and use their popularity, influence and position to rally people to an unpopular change process so that an organisation is reformed and improved. They could have easily gone with the anti-change crowd, but didn't.

You will know what I mean when you see the opposite: a group of people who vehemently resist any change that discommodes their personal set-up and who in their opposition adopt such toxic behaviours that they also leave a legacy – one of discord and a broken system that sets their service back years.

Leaving a legacy means leaving something new or improved behind you: innovations, enhanced relationships, new systems, extraordinary levels of service, excellence in standards, or buoyant morale, something over and above the job description. The key is to do this now before life slips by.

## From positioning to sparkling

I believe that standing up and giving an excellent speech with no notes is the way to really position your personal brand as outstanding.

It is an excellent move to speak within the company, as mentioned earlier, but it shifts it to a whole new level if you seek opportunities to speak at outside events and conferences. I have a number of clients who have made speaking opportunities at national conferences and international events a key part of their brand positioning.

### Be a master at speaking

Clearly, if you want to succeed in business today, you must be able to speak in front of your colleagues. There is no doubt that standing up and making a presentation sets you apart. However, when it comes to positioning, I'm talking about going one step further and speaking on the stage at large gatherings of people – keynote speaking.

This is a double-edged sword because you stand out, but many executives do such a poor job of it that they stand out for the wrong reasons. There is a lot spoken about fear of speaking in public and it being more frightening than death. Granted it is a challenge, but not insurmountable. You need to get over it. Believe me, I have trained the most frightened of people. It is not something you develop in one day or because someone sprinkled "magic speaking dust" on you. If you approach it in a logical way and spend time developing the skill, you will succeed.

To achieve stand-out positioning, I want you to get yourself speaking opportunities and aim to stand in the middle of the stage, speak for 45 minutes with no notes and get a huge round of applause, and make a memorable impression. Be the most talked about speaker at any event where you speak.

### NOIRÍN: EXCELLENT SPEAKERS SPARKLE

I met Noirín when she was beginning to position her personal brand by making presentations at company events and offering to chair or MC internal events. I was invited to an event her company was running at which she was the master of ceremonies. I sat in the audience, dumbfounded at how she changed when she got onto the stage. She mumbled and read her words from an A4 piece of paper flapping in her hands. Her public relations agency had written the introduction for her, in their words not hers. She had not read it beforehand, and so she stumbled over the unfamiliar words. I witnessed this powerful, intelligent, dynamic woman make a shockingly bad impression on the room. She was wooden, had no eye contact and looked like an amateur. All of her dynamism had evaporated. Remember I told you about leaking power earlier? Well, this was a horrible example of a woman leaking all her power into the audience.

It was in that moment that I realised that every conversation about personal branding must address the issue of public speaking. Because she was such an impressive person, I challenged her to work on her public speaking skills. She was an example of someone with a wonderful personal brand who could take it to the next level very easily. So she set herself the aim of making a 45-minute speech to an industry conference in six months' time.

We worked on what I call her 'killer' speech for some time. Our aim was that she would be able to stand in the middle of the stage, speak for the 45 minutes without notes, get a huge round of applause, and be quoted afterwards. She found a speaking opportunity and we worked on her speech. She went on to give the same speech five times to different audiences. The more she gave the speech, the more comfortable she became in her own skin. This is a great idea as you get more and more comfortable with the content and the ability to read the audience's reaction to your content and delivery. You should see her now, she walks onto the stage, commands it, and because she gives this impressive performance every time, she stands out. She is often asked to speak at conferences and this has brought her to the attention of the influential people she needs to impress to further her career.

## Positioning is vital

Positioning is the final step in building your personal brand. It is no use concentrating only on building the first seven steps, where you learn about yourself and what others think of you, develop an ambitious career plan, modify your behaviours and hold your power, then forgetting the last step and staying stuck in one very small part of the company. You run the risk of being a "legend in your own garage"!

You must always have an eye on how your brand is positioned and how that position changes. Get the basics correct, always aim to go beyond merely participating and find ways to be a contributor. Be constantly aware of the five principles of positioning and give serious thought to your positioning strategy. As you develop in your career and become more experienced, and hopefully more senior, you really do need to take care and time to work on being a charismatic leader and go beyond the basics to carve out a place as a thought leader.

There is much I could write on the topic of sparkling in your career and I cannot emphasise enough how being a really accomplished speaker is one of the surest ways of achieving that. I feel so strongly about this that I think I may write my next book on how to speak in public for 45 minutes without notes!

# The final step: steppin' out with your new personal brand

At this stage you might be wondering how you are going to make your personal brand work for the rest of your career. I would like to tell you about one final step to guarantee that all your hard work on building your personal brand will not fade over time, but will become an integral part of your continued career success.

At this point in the process you have done the exercises, read the case studies and reflected. You have an excellent understanding of each of the eight components of the model, and have gone through each step in sequence. The most important and career-defining step is now in front of you. It is only possible to do this when you are totally familiar with the individual steps.

The final step is when you integrate all the previous steps into a responsive model and bring it to life, using it as a whole and not just the sum of its parts.

In explaining how this works, I use the analogy of learning to drive. Remember when you first sat in the driving seat and had to learn separately about the gear stick, the clutch, the brakes, the indicators and how you had to master each of these, and you wondered how you could ever pull it all together? You timidly left the safety of an empty car park early on a Sunday morning and ventured out onto the back roads, and you began to integrate all of the components and drive slowly, but you were driving! Fast-forward to when you no longer saw each component as a separate entity, because you had developed an integrated view of all of them, and now moved effortlessly between them. You made it out on to the motorway, and only when you are faced with a particular danger did you think about individual components, like braking on icy roads, or using the correct lights in a fog. Using the personal brand model is a similar process. You unconsciously move between each step of the model as you progress through your career.

Before we move to the final step, let's remind ourselves of the model as a whole.

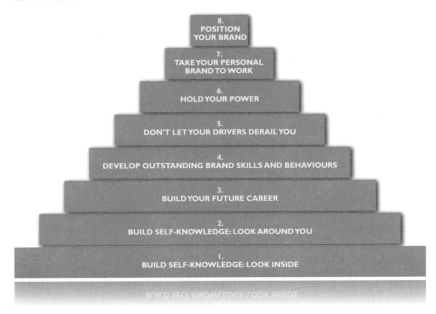

Of course, you need to keep a watchful eye over the individual components that make up your personal brand. However, there are two further aspects that you need to be constantly aware of as you refine your personal brand through your evolving career:

1. To keep your personal brand powerful, you need to **integrate** the eight interlocking elements to create a synergy between them. Be aware of the knock-on effect of the elements.
2. As you evolve through the different stages of your career, you need to keep your personal brand **responsive** and relevant at all times.

## 1. The power of integration

At different stages in your career you will find that one of the eight steps of the model can be more pressing than the others. At this stage, it is vital to realise that a change in any of the eight steps has a knock-on effect on the others, because all the steps are interconnected. Look below at how a change in one can affect all the others.

### Self-knowledge

As you progress through your career, you will learn more about yourself as you get constant feedback from others, and so your view changes. If you discover that you have a new interest or that you are particularly good at some activity, this may affect your career plans. This will also cause you to look to widen your matrix, which will then affect your positioning plan.

## Build your future career

If you decide that you want to leave your present company, the milestones in your career plan will shift and your matrix will change. You'll have to look again at your skill-set and your behaviours and plan to change all of them in some way.

## Your behaviours

If you find that your behaviour in work is changing due to increased responsibility, personal challenges, change of boss or teammates, you may see that this new behaviour is derailing you. This may affect how others see you, and can have an adverse effect on your career progression.

## Your matrix

A big change in your work environment, like a merger, takeover or change of company leadership with arrival of new senior personnel, can transform your matrix. This then affects your positioning plans, meaning that you may have to adapt your behaviours to fit into a new company culture. Certain behaviours that were customary under the previous regime may no longer be acceptable.

## Integration in action

Imagine you have built a purposeful brand. You understand your strengths and weaknesses, you've behaved in a way that has brought you to the attention of the important people in your matrix, you've positioned yourself, and you're now ready for the next milestone in your career – your Big Audacious Aim.

You may have moved from one division of the company to another, but now find yourself working with someone whose leadership behaviours you find very difficult, and who is now in charge of your destiny for the coming year. What I would like you to do in this circumstance is to review all of the components of your personal brand. Start with another look at yourself and try to understand more fully what it is about this situation that is diminishing your ability. Envisage how you appear to other people as you struggle with this, and query if your behaviour is also contributing to the situation. Ask yourself if, as a consequence, you are derailing your career.

It could be that you have been promoted to lead a team of people among whom you were previously considered an equal, but now you are the manager. The prospects of the company have deteriorated and now you have to lead increased productivity initiatives. You run the risk of being seen as the 'big bad boss', so you need to revisit your self-knowledge and ask yourself the following: are you equipped to deal with this changed relationship? How do you feel about managing conflicts? Does this derail you? How does this new pressure in your life affect how you appear to your superiors in your matrix? Is this going to damage your brand and stall your further progression? Again, you will need to revisit all eight components individually and be conscious of the potential knock-on effect that a change in one can have on the others.

## 2. Responsiveness

Although working on the interconnection is vital, this alone is not enough. You need also need to make your integrated brand responsive to the constant changes in your work environment.

Your work should not end when you have built the model – it will not stay relevant if it is static. You need to be aware that your career is changing all the time: you change and your environment changes. If you are working in a fast-paced company, you need to be very responsive if you are to take advantage and progress your career. If you do not constantly evolve your personal brand and make yourself relevant, there is a real danger you will be left behind.

When you see a promotion opportunity, you need to respond by systematically stepping up each aspect of the model to the next level. A good rule is to benchmark against a position two steps up from your circumstance. As you seek promotion, you need to be aware that your personal brand now needs to be that of somebody two steps up. In addition, you need to create a higher, wider matrix, become first-class at positioning and have best-in-class behaviours, with no possibility of them derailing you. Remember, this is built on an accurate knowledge of yourself and a steadfast determination to work the milestones necessary to get to your Big Audacious Aim.

**PATRICK: MAKE YOUR PERSONAL BRAND
CENTRAL TO YOUR CAREER**

Patrick is a 40-something executive who I have worked with for the past number of years. He has changed position and moved country during that time and he is a wonderful example of someone who has built a truly integrated and responsive personal brand.

When I met him, I was his first executive mentor. He had very little self-knowledge and spent no time on self-reflection. He was stalled in his career and was engaging in some behaviour that was derailing him. He was very ambitious and a workaholic; his insistence that all his staff keep up with his frantic work rate alienated many and caused them to complain about him.

We worked through all the components of the model and he did all the exercises, and the end of our first programme together coincided with his move out of Ireland. He had the chance to operate his personal brand in a totally new environment.

No one had any previous idea about Patrick and had never seen his previous work style. This experience allowed him to work at integrating all the components. He deepened his self-knowledge as he had to learn to live and work in a new country, in a new company, and in a new sector of business. It was a huge learning opportunity!

Patrick up-skilled and made sure that no derailing behaviours stalled him. He increased his listening skills and really worked on developing empathy. He consciously held on to his power, avoiding his previous power-leaking behaviours, and he learnt his matrix management in the new job.

After two years, Patrick came back to Ireland at a higher position and again worked his personal brand in another new company. He was very proficient at positioning at this stage, having successfully navigated his return to a prestigious company in Ireland.

In summary, Patrick's conviction that his personal brand drives his career means that he constantly works on analysing himself and what he is thinking and doing. His desire to grow, his love of self-discovery and lifelong learning have propelled his career. He is alert to what is going on around him within his matrix, and so is very conscious of behaviours and sets of circumstances that could derail him.

This self-awareness, professional detachment and devotion to excellence which he has crafted in addition to being a hardworking, intelligent person, has marked Patrick out in the company. He has become a role model, and his employers send him to their offices around the world so that other people can benchmark off his innovative ideas and ways of working.

Patrick has actually built the personal brand of somebody with enormous personal potential and a great ability to transform people around him.

Finally, my concluding thoughts are that I am utterly convinced that the eight steps presented here, when worked together, will allow you to develop an extremely powerful, purposeful personal brand. Your brand will be seen by others as a truly defining quality in what is an extremely competitive market, and will help advance your career to the highest level.

Good luck,
Veronica

# Suggested Further Reading

Arbinger Institute, *Leadership and Self-Deception: Getting out of the Box* (Berrett-Koehler Publishers, 2010).

Canning, Veronica, *Shoeisms: Working Woman's Guide to Take Control and be the Sassy, Successful Woman You Know You Can Be* (Morgan James Publishing, 2009).

Carter, Jay, *Nasty People: How to Stop Being Hurt by Them without Stooping to Their Level* (McGraw-Hill, 2003).

Goleman, Daniel, *Emotional Intelligence: Why It Can Matter More Than IQ* (Bantam Books, 2005).

Hare, Robert and Paul Babiak, *Snakes in Suits: When Psychopaths Go to Work* (HarperBusiness, 2007).

James, Oliver, *Office Politics: How to Thrive in a World of Lying, Backstabbing and Dirty Tricks* (Vermillion, 2013).

Kahneman, Daniel, *Thinking, Fast and Slow* (Penguin, 2012).

Seligman, Martin, *Flourish: A Visionary New Understanding of Happiness and Well-being* (Atria Books, 2012).

Truss, Lynne, *Eats, Shoots & Leaves: The Zero Tolerance Approach to Punctuation* (Prospect Books, 2003).

# About the author

An internationally acclaimed speaker, consultant and author, Veronica Canning is a much sought after business mentor who has 30 years' experience of working at senior level in a wide range of companies.

Veronica works with business people in blue chip organisations, addressing their challenges, including developing an executive presence and building or repairing their personal brands. Applying her considerable practical experience when she works on a one-to-one basis, she has worked with a broad range of people to develop outstanding personal brands.

Companies work with Veronica to develop their high-potential managers, and rely on her discretion and experience to guide them in identifying possible barriers to their success and then finding solutions. She helps people to understand and reframe their challenges through developing an in-depth understanding of themselves and others, their points of view, motivations and reactions. In particular, she works with people who have high potential but are jeopardising their careers by their behaviours and the unwitting damage they do to their personal brands. A hallmark of her approach is her ability to encourage people to make ambitious plans for their future and to fulfil those ambitions.

As well as her work with individuals, Veronica has designed many group programmes, customised to the organisation's exact challenge. She has worked across all sectors and sizes of enterprise, including SMEs, multinationals and public sector organisations. Veronica has worked with the EU in Bosnia, rolling out one of her customised programmes for key leadership figures in the post-war reconstruction effort.

Veronica is also an expert motivational speaker and in recent years has spoken widely to senior executives and entrepreneurs. She has extensive media experience and ran a business-based radio series in 2012, in which she interviewed senior executives from a range of industries on key business issues.

As a business executive, Veronica has travelled extensively both in her work with Trocaire and the Red Cross. As a speaker, she is highly sought after for her motivational speeches on personal performance and business issues, most recently addressing audiences in Dubai and China. She is a past President of the Professional Speakers Association of Ireland, a member of the Global Speakers Federation, a member of the Institute of Directors in Ireland and was the first Mentor for the Canadian Women's Executive Network in Ireland.

# What others having been saying about YOU® BRAND

*"Veronica has a transformative effect on those that work with her. She encourages a deep self-knowledge. In this book she shares her insights and reading it creates a path to career success."*

St. John O'Gara, FCA, Group CEO, Tazbell Services

*"Veronica Canning is someone I have worked with on and off for a number of years. In all of the assignments she has undertaken for me, she has demonstrated a depth of expertise and ability to adapt to the needs of each situation with consummate professionalism. She does so with a sense of calm and in a way that gets to the heart of the issue at hand ... this insightful and pragmatic approach is what, for me, makes Veronica a valued and respected support even in the most challenging of circumstances. I am delighted to see Veronica put into words her own creative and thought-provoking views in relation to a subject I know she is passionate about."*

John Keogh, Global HR, Bristol-Myers Squibb

*"Written by a master of people motivation, YOU® BRAND explores what makes a person successful in their career and gives you solid, immediately actionable advice to make you more successful. This book leaves you with a great feeling of confidence, ambition and the eight steps needed to build a successful career. When you read this book you will move your career up a step while also remembering one important principle in life: your personal brand is not what you say it is; it's what others say about you."*

Mary Duff, Director of Nursing,
St Vincent's University Hospital, Dublin;
Adjunct Associate Professor of Nursing,
UCD, University Hospital

*"In this wonderful book Veronica Canning gives us a practical, easily usable model to build a powerful personal brand. I really recommend it to anyone who wants to break free of their limitations and move forward significantly in their career. It is a guidebook for taking personal responsibility for your effect on others and for you to achieve success. Buy it. Read it. You will be glad you did."*

Caroline Curtis, FCCA,
VP Finance International, Nuance Communications Ireland

*"Take up Veronica's challenge. What have you got to lose? Doing something to discover your true self and equipping yourself with the tools to succeed is always worth your time. Veronica has provided all the steps you need to get your career moving again to where you expect it to be. Go for it!"*

Alan McGilton, Insurance Executive,
Management Consultant and Ethics Lecturer

*"Never before were so many people expected to manage their own careers and never before did people have so many options in front of them. But with greater freedom may come a greater stress and the feeling of 'we can do more with our lives'. Veronica Canning's new book, YOU® BRAND, aims at helping those who want to get more out of their working lives. Through systematic building blocks, the book helps individuals increase their awareness of how they appear to the outside world and explains how to build an image and manage it both internally and externally in order to capitalise better on their professional assets.*

*One of the sentences in Veronica's book that resonated with me was 'For it to succeed and contribute to your development it must be authentic.' Thus, the lesson that Veronica teaches is not how to create a fictitious and superficial 'new self' in order to appeal to others but rather how to find that richer and deeper inner self that can enrich one's life as well as others.*

*Veronica's book would be a very useful companion for anyone who wants to gain a clearer understanding of their professional identity as well as their external image, giving practical and applicable advice on how to manage one's brand to bring about a higher level of professional satisfaction."*

Dr Jacob Eisenberg, Academic Director of
MSc Business Programmes,
UCD Michael Smurfit Graduate Business School